THE PHILOSOPHY OF GOD

JDV Philosophy Series - 10

THE PHILOSOPHY OF GOD

Faith and Traditions

Cyril Desbruslais SJ

Edited By

Kuruvilla Pandikattu, SJ

Jnana-Deepa Vidyapeeth

&

Christian World Imprints

First Published in 2019 by

Jnana-Deepa Vidyapeeth
Ramwadi, Nagar Road, **Pune-411014**
jdvoffice@jdv.edu.in
www.jdv.edu.in
Phone: +91 20 41036111

&

Christian World Imprints
Christian Publishing & Books from India
C-3, Shop No. 14, Ground Floor
Wazirpur Industrial Area, **Delhi-110052**
cwidelhi2017@gmail.com
www.ChristianWorldImprints.com
Phone: +91 11 41526079

ISBN: 978-93-5148-377-9 (HB)
ISBN: 978-93-5148-378-6 (PB)

"Published with the help of the Institute of Missiology – Germany"

Printed in India.

CONTENTS

JDV PHILOSOPHY SERIES - 10

Since 1893 Jnana-Deepa Vidyapeeth has been pioneering philosophy discussion and debate inspired by prominent personalities like Richard De Smet, Jean de Marneffe, Salvino Azzopardi, Cyril Desbruslais, Noel Sheth, John Vattanky, etc. It has been in the forefront of promoting Indian philosophy and making philosophical thinking relevant for contemporary times. In its effort to reach out to like-minded scholars, JDV Philosophy Series has been visualized as a catalyst for interdisciplinary thinking and contemporary exploration on social issues fostering holistic liberation, integral development and creative engagement.

JDV Philosophy Series

1. Salvino Azzopardi: ***Epistemology and Phenomenology of Religions*** (2018)
2. Kuruvilla Pandikattu & Thomas Karimundackal (eds): ***Melodies from the Flute*** (2018)
3. Kurien Kunnumpuram: ***Freedom and Joy*** (2018)
4. Cyril Desbruslais SJ: ***Postmodernity: An Indian Christian Philosophical Appraisal*** (2019)
5. Cyril Desbruslais SJ: ***Metaphysics Philosophy of Be-ing for Today*** (2019)
6. John Peter Vallabadoss: ***Indian Thinkers: Modern and Contemporary Period*** (2019)
7. Thomas Karimundackal & Kuruvilla Pandikattu (eds): ***Logic and Love***: For Prof John Vattanky SJ (2019)
8. Fabian Jose UMI: ***Relevance of Thomas Merton's Spirituality for the Consecrated Life in India*** (2019)
9. Kuruvilla Pandikattu & PT Mathew (eds): ***Committed to the Church and the Country***: For Prof Kurien Kunnumpuam SJ (2019)
10. Cyril Desbruslais SJ: ***The Philosophy of God for Today*** (2019)

Chapter 1

INTRODUCTORY ISSUES

a. Philosophy in General

Etymologically, the word *philosophy* comes from two Greek words – *philos,* lover (or friend) and *sophia*, wisdom. Philosophy, then, is "a love of wisdom" and the philosopher is a friend or a lover of wisdom.

Some important conclusions can already be drawn from this fact. Philosophy is not the *possession* of wisdom, a philosopher is NOT a proud Mr Know-It-All, who has all of the answers to everyone's questions. He is a quester after truth, profoundly in love with *Sophia*, pursuing her, but never quite able to comprehend her elusive person. At most, he touches her with his finger-tips, but she soon escapes his grasp.[1]

From this we could emphasise that humility would be the first necessary qualification of any philosopher worth his/her salt. A philosopher is one who treks a weary, but ever so exciting and adventurous, way along paths less trod to an ever-receding horizon. The truth is there, but is always, tantalisingly, just beyond his/her reach. A good philosopher leads us one step nearer to the truth but is never so smug as to claim that we have ensnared Dame Sophia once and for all in the meshes of human finite intelligence!

We might even go on to say that philosophy must be a community project. There is **only so much** that an individual human mind can grasp. Reality is far too rich, far too complex to be stuffed into the slender limits of one individual – brain, be it that of Mme Curie or Herr Einstein! Besides,

1 I apologise for the sexist-sounding implications of my words! It Would Seem That I Am Implying Only Males Can Be Philosophers – As I Have Reserved The Pronoun, "He" To Indicate The Philosopher. My Only Excuse Is That I Want To Use The Image Of Lover And Beloved Frequently In This Text And *Sophia*, Besides Being Feminine In Greek, Is A Very Common Girl's Name In Many Languages. So ...

each of us approaches persons and things from our particular perspective (some have called this the "pre-understanding"), which comprises, among other things, our individual culture, our mother-tongue, family upbringing, religious background (even if we think we have rejected it long ago). All these, somehow or the other, influence (if not prejudice) our perceptions. It is impossible to take a totally neutral,unbiased view of things: at best we can try to become progressively more aware of our "pre-understanding" and give up naive assumptions about objectivity. As we shall see, I am not saying that we can know nothing objectively; I am, rather, asking us to be on guard against hasty and presumptuous assertions that we have come to a plain, unvarnished and objective visions of reality. Whatever, it should be quite clear that none of us deliberately and wilfully admits prejudices into our perceptual make-up. People hold prejudices unconsciously, as a rule: once they become conscious of the fact that they have been nurturing prejudices, they give them up (assuming they have the honesty and courage to do so). But, how can we become aware of our prejudices? Only by dialoguing with people of other backgrounds (other nations, other cultures, other creeds). If I sequester myself with people who think exactly as I do and never venture to meet people with other worldviews, I and my gifting will simply confirm each other in our favourite prejudices and narrow mindednesses!

b. Philosophy and Science

For quite some time, especially since the advent of the scientific age, philosophy has had a bad press. In fact, many philosophers themselves (including the "father of modern philosophy, Rene Descartes 1596 – 1650) lamented because philosophy lacked the precision and certainty of mathematics. At the turn of the last century, Edmund Husserl was still dreaming of a philosophy that would be an "exact science", yielding unquestionable certainty based on indubitable evidence and proofs. And it does look as if philosophy is a kind of third rate discipline, since – as we have said above – it cannot give us guaranteed "once and for all" exact answers. But is this really such a blemish? Let us take a closer look at the issue.

I may borrow an insight from the contemporary French existentialist thinker Gabriel Marcel (1889-1973), we should make a clear distinction between problems and mysteries (even though, in popular speech we use them almost interchangeably): a problem is a question of which I am not a part, whereas a mystery is a question of which I am a part. For example, take the question, "What is the chemical composition of table salt?" I am not part of that question, so it is a problem. However, the question, "Is there such a thing as true love?" or "Is there life after death?" These are mystery-questions because they concern me, personally. True love and life after death are issues with which my life is intimately bound up. Even the question, "Does God exist?" or even, "What is God like?" are mystery-questions – not because I am trying to say that I am part of God, but because if God exists then I would somehow be very intimately linked with the divinity. So far, we've noted how problem and mystery differ from the point of view of the kind of question they ask. Let us move on to their answers.

Precisely because I am not part of a problem-question, I can detach myself from it, observe it objectively,' submit it to experiments in the laboratory or elsewhere and, given enough time and equipment, work out a final, exhaustive, once-and-for-all answer. But, I cannot do that with a mystery- question; in as much as I am part of it, I cannot detach myself from it any more than I can detach myself from myself. That is why I cannot, in *principle*. ever work out that kind of answer for a mystery. Science is busy with problems: that is why science can attain a high level of certainty and demonstration or proof (though even scientists, nowadays, are not so cocksure about their "certainties"). Philosophy (like theology and religion) is busy with mysteries and that is why it can, at best, throw some more light on the complexities of the issue, no more. It should be clear, critical and coherent.

But this does not mean that philosophy (or theology, or religion) are irresponsible and whimsical subjects to be pursued by dilettantes according to their fads and fancies. Even if its responses cannot partake of that level of absolute certainty that the positive sciences (allegedly) claim, it has to be orderly, painstaking and observant as any other study. It has to be critical of its presuppositions and pre-understanding, submit all its reasoning to the strict canons of logic and so on. Philosophy is not a science, but it is a systematic scientific discipline.

c. Religion in General

Religion is one of those words that dictionaries tell us have an unknown or doubtful etymology. There is a Latin word *religare* (to tie up again) which is the closest contender for its source, but that is highly doubtful. Is this meant to tell us that religion is a set of rules and regulations that bind us up again, after the civil code has finished enmeshing us? This would imply a very legalistic and uninspiring understanding of religion, indeed – one that would hardly inspire much commitment from most of us. Theology is, a kind of close relative of it and it means, literally, God-talk. In practice, however, theology is usually associated with the study of some allegedly revealed book. Thus, Christian theology takes off from the *Bible*. Jewish theology starts from the *Torah*. Islamic theology studies the *Koran*. Hindu theology **delves** into, say, the *Gita* and so on. However, it would not be quite correct to link all religions with some scripture claimed to be divinely revealed, for there are many tribal religions without a "holy book" – other than the Great Book of Nature in which God stands revealed to His people. Indeed, not all religions even accept the notion of God. At least two religions, Jainism and one school of Buddhism reject the whole idea of God (i.e. they are atheistic)!

What, then, is the most basic idea common to all religions? It is the idea of the sacred. Various authors have tried to give a rough summary definition of this as the wholly other (*ganz Andere*). the highly powerful (and hence dangerous – high voltage, do not touch!) and so on. In general, there seems to come a time when we suddenly become convinced that there is more to life than all that we can merely see or hear or touch or smell or feel. This can happen when one is caught up in the mystery of child-birth: when a young mother holds in her exhausted arms the first baby she's even given birth to or when the proud and humble father holds in his trembling arms his tiny firstborn; or when one stands on the seashore and contemplates the mighty ocean ' rolling back and forth; or when one-is hushed by the panorama of natural and serene beauty that lies exposed from-a lofty mountain-top} or ... in so much other cases where powerful emotions of love or anger or joy or resolve overwhelm us. Out of this arises the experience of the Sacred which some of us interpret as but an aspect of ourselves ("the human shadow writ large"). But others remain equally convinced that it is a genuine experience of the Divine.

There is also the idea of salvation or liberation which is common to all religions, though it may be understood very differently. Don't we all feel, when we read the papers or watch TV that "the time is out of joint" that something has gone wrong, horribly wrong, with the world? Don't we all dream of a-world of justice and love and peace, where all people will live in harmony as brothers and sisters and not bully or terrorise various groups on the basis of ethnic or other differences? And do not even the best of us recognise within ourselves what psychologists call a "shadow side", a strange inner urge to cheat and steal, to take the line of least resistance, to lie and exploit others. Very often we fight against these mysterious promptings ("temptations", as some prefer to call them)? Oftentimes we give in, due to pressure of circumstances, peer influence or plain and simple cowardice and laziness. All religions offer us various ways and means to overcome these unpleasant tendencies: they offer us guidance and advise us to try meditation, prayer and other ways to control our passions and less healthy drives.

Finally, all religions are communitarian expressions. Indeed, religions emerge when people come together, share their experiences and, somehow or the other, arrive at certain- helpful structures which bind them to each other and facilitate the expression and celebration of their common vision. Thus religions, as communitarian expressions of shared convictions, become structured or institutionalised. But this is what makes many serious-minded and sincerely religious people baulk at religion, or to put it more precisely, at the highly organised and formal religious set-ups that they are confronted with. Is it really necessary to pray and worship according to these strict and impersonal structures? Wouldn't it be more fulfilling, spontaneous and meaningful to do it quietly at home? And do we need to be bossed about by "religious leaders", a pack of conservative old fuddy-duddies, arrogant, domineering, power-hungry ... and often money-mad? This is a question we will have to go into very shortly!

d. Philosophy of Religion

For some people, the very idea of philosophising about religion is blasphemy! Isn't it a form of the most crass arrogance and irreligiosity to submit the notion of the Sacred, of God and of Holy Writ to the critical probings of finite, limited human intelligence? Would not the only appropriate human response to the experience of the Sacred be humble, silent and respectful submission and adoration? In the West, Martin Luther (1483-1546), the fiery German reformer, spear-headed this approach, fulminating against reason as "the devil's greatest whore", averring that it "can do nothing but shame and disgrace all that God says and does". For him there was a mortal enmity between faith and reason: "Faith strikes dead this reason, and kills this beast, which heaven and earth and all creatures cannot destroy." Among Eastern thinkers who have championed such a view, perhaps the most outspoken was the medieval Islamic scholar and mystic Algazel or Ghazali (1059-1111) who, in his *The Destruction of Philosophers*[2] tells us, in no uncertain terms, what he thought of those who used reason in the course of their search for God. Thomas Aquinas (1225-1274), later canonised by the Catholic Church, was more positive in his attitude towards reason and philosophy in the context of religion though he was no "crass rationalist". The same, too, could be said of Ibn Sina (980-1036), whose name was Latinised into Avicenna by the Scholastics and whom Algazel saw as his arch-enemy, co-religionist of his though he was!

Extreme polarisations are seldom productive and this is quite true of the "pure reason" vs "blind faith" clash over religion. The "faith alone" approach opens the door to uncritical, self-deluded psychotics and fanatics. But "reason alone" is no improvement. Absolute rationalism ("I'll only accept what can stand up to a rigorous proof!) is both impractical and irrational. Among other things it would exclude any possibility of inter-personal relationships, like love and friendship and not only religions faith! An absolute rationalist, were he or she to act consistently, would be condemned to a lonely, loveless and friendless (and not just 'religious faithless') life! And, just for the record, it is interesting to note that the Catholic Church has officially condemned, as heresies, both of these attitudes: "fideism" (faith alone) and "exaggerated rationalism" (reason alone). From the preceding, we can conclude that the most appropriate response

---

2 Ghazzālī, and Sabih A. Kamali. *Ghazālī'stahāfut Al-Falāsifah (destruction of the Philosophers)*, 1955.

would be a balanced "mid-point-between-the-two- extremes" approach, which I would venture to designate as "reasonable risk". Indeed, this is what we do to validate any inter-personal commitment, including love and friendship and not only religious faith. We establish some demonstrable grounds to justify our commitment. However, since we are dealing with free persons and their invisible interior lives, there can never be a fool-proof guarantee as to the certainty and security of the commitment one is making. There is a solid basis of reasonableness, but not absolute rationality. The commitment is not grounded on blind risk: there is some evidence in favour of one's personal commitment! it can stand up to considerable critical inquisition. Yet the possibility of being mistaken is not totally ruled out: hence, there is an element of risk. It is neither unfounded risk nor indubitable argument, but halfway between both, drawing upon the strengths of each to avoid the excesses of either.

e. But Do We Need (Organised-Religion, Really?)

Let us begin by admitting the fact that, historically, no organised religion can stand up to honest criticism and come out of it with an unblemished report card. None of the mainline religions has proved itself to have been always and everywhere a reliable[1] friend of people struggling for liberation and emancipation. Often religions have added to the oppression, discrimination and blood-letting that have plagued the world since time began. The subjugation of women has often been given religious sanction. The most cruel and blood thirsty wars have been inspired by religious differences, with each side proclaiming an exclusive *Gott mit uns!* (God is with us!) while hailing all opponents as hirelings of Satan incarnate. Religion has often opposed scientific research and sided with obscurantism and superstition, against trends of enlightenment. And politicians, especially in Third World countries, have learned that religion is the easiest handle with which to manipulate impoverished and oppressed masses, stirring up all kinds of mob violence and building up their "vote banks"! Indeed, religious leadership seems to be the last bastion of male exclusivism, determined to hold out against "female incursions" by all manner of pseudo theological, philosophical and sociological argument, so as to preserve power in the hands of men only. The priestly Conquerors? Club is a very powerful and jealously guarded coterie of old men who, with bulldog tenacity, clings with alarm to its ever shrinking list of "privileges and prerogatives."

Above all, it stands ready to flash its magic wand of "God's Will" and "the divinely established scheme of things" to justify and protect the status quo (heavily loaded in its favour) and block any attempt at reform which just might, among other things, help towards a more authentic encounter with God.

On the other hand, (there always is another hand, isn't it?) religions have alsoinspired many to selfless service of the downtrodden, have given the human race a rich legacy of art and beauty as well as played a not insignificant role in opening our eyes to the essential dignity of the human person, irrespective of race, colour or sex; Some religious personalities – Mother Teresa, Dorothy Day, Mahatma Gandhi, Oscar Romero, Desmond Tutu – have been true friends to liberation movements.

Yet, when all is said and done, it would appear that some kind of institutionalisation or organisation of religion is inevitable – unless we are quite prepared to accept the consequences of reducing it to some sort of private, abstract and "spiritual" preoccupation. In fact, we can cite at least three major reasons why some kind of organisation in religion is not merely to be tolerated as unavoidable, but even accepted as inevitable.

First, inasmuch as we are embodied beings, we cannot be satisfied with an intangible something, which remains at that level. Anything that we take seriously must be embodied, "tangibilised" in some way, through some manner of institutionalisation, just as our love for our country has to be given tangible expression in flag-hoistings and march-pasts and our love for our family and friends has to be rendered incarnate in birthday parties and family gatherings. Anything less would but touch us lightly and leave us with a profound sense of frustration. Secondly, if religion is to have some social significance, if it is to have some transformative, reformative impact upon society – inspiring people to work for justice and peace, or in support of the environment – it requires some kind of communitarian expression. Finally, if it is not to become a fleeting, fly-by-night sort of thing, here today and gone tomorrow, coming to birth and dying with each individual's alleged encounter with the powers that be, it must have some concrete form to ensure the sharing, preservation and development of its tradition.

Actually, if we look a bit- more closely at the objections against organised religion, it would probably become clear that these are not so much aimed at the very *fact* that religions are organised, but at the rigid,' authoritarian *way* in which they have been organised. *That* is the real villain!

f. A Timely Qualification

I have maintained that organised religion is somehow inevitable and, even more, that it is not a bad thing. Indeed, there is no reason why we can't envisage institutionalised religions being organised in a more "user-friendly", democratic and less authoritarian way. Religions should encourage us to respect other traditions, religious or otherwise, learn from their insights and promote unity in diversity in lieu of upholding a soulless, monotonous uniformity.

In other words, my recognition of the necessity of organised religion does not by any means, imply that I give my whole-hearted and uncritical support to the actual way in which contemporary institutionalised religions are, in fact, organised! Far from it. And when, later, I use terms like "oppressive" and "liberative" when speaking of concrete religious set-ups in today's world, I will not be insinuating that any one particular religion and its structures are liberative and to be encouraged, while that of all others is simply oppressive and to be resisted. My contention is that every organised religion is susceptible of a liberative and an oppressive interpretation. Indeed, there is even such a thing as oppressive and liberative atheism. It's all a question as to whether the atheist or believer is ultimately seeking the enhancement and development of the entire human person or not. It's this that makes all the difference.

g. The Three "C's" of Organised Religion

The basis of authentic religion is a personal and mystical encounter with God, the *ganz Andere* or "whatever be ones preferred description of whatever is experienced in religious activity. Nor is this "mystical experience" as esoteric and unattainable as many people think. All that it requires, on our part, is a pre-disposing attitude of humility, of openness, "the heart of a little child." And this is difficult because it is so easy. The more we consider ourselves "religiously learned", the more meticulous we are in performing our "religious duties", the bigger is the occupational hazard of mistaking the pointing finger for the moon, not to mention the hazard of falling into spiritual pride or intolerance! In fact, it is the religious fanatic – whose mind and heart is too far removed from that of a little child to be open to any genuine encounter with the *ganz Andere* – who invariably becomes the self-appointed, overzealous and merciless enforcer of the rigid observance of the unholy trinity of code-creed-cult, which is his (deliberate choice of the masculine) tyrannical substitute divinity. And the religious fanatic is basically unsure of his convictions: that is why he has to burn, maim or blow up those who don't reduplicate his approach. The existence of people who see or think differently from him is a threat to his own insecure vision!

Creed is a kind of summary list of the particular doctrines to which all would' be followers of a specific religion are required to give their unqualified, assent. In a very tightly organised religion, failure to do so would invite unpleasant repercussions. To begin with, one would be hailed a "heretic", "schismatic", "infidel", "gentile" or whatever be the current term of opprobrium in the reigning fanatics' vocabulary. Once upon a time, such qualification would have resulted in one's death sentence: being carted off to the stake in an *auto da fé*,[3] stoned, hanged-drawn-and-quartered, removed from the land of the living by some form of ostracism, excommunication, a *fatwah* or, another ingenious and efficacious means of silencing dissent. In our more "enlightened" times, the fanatic has to settle for more "civilised"

3 This refers to the burning of a heretic by the Spanish Inquisition, which lasted roughly 700 years. The official start is usually given as 1231 A.D., when the pope appoints the first "inquisitors of heretical depravity." The Spanish Inquisition, which begins under Ferdinand and Isabella, doesn't end until the 19th century — the last execution was in 1826.

and, "unbloody" devices: censure, withdrawal of one's licence to teach, banning and/ or burning of ones books... Of course, the believing community has every right to judge which enunciations of faith-convictions authentically express the commonly held convictions of the general body of the faithful. But it should be the community, or a truly representative body of it, that sees, judges and acts – not an over-centralised, over-aged conservative and all-male select band of people with vested interests, closed to all other points of view or perspectives. Such executive-legislative-judiciary power should not be allowed to be monopolised by a small, inbreeding Conquerors' Club, jealous of its power and position!

Code comprises all those moral rules and derived customs that followers of a particular organised religion are supposed to live by, day to day. These may include styles of dress, dietary prescriptions, allotted "holy days" for worship, "penitential times" for fasting, and so on. Most religions seem to agree on basic moral principles as respect for elders, no stealing and the like. There is a difference of opinion, however, as regards certain issues on sex, such as birth-control and some other areas, as the use of violence, even in times of war and so on. There was a time when all religions were so intimately linked with State policy, that any contravention of the religious code was considered a treasonous act against the State and the culprit was turned over to the secular arm for punishment. Nowadays, most religions have – voluntarily or reluctantly relinquished such links and have had to content themselves with merely issuing moral condemnations against offenders, warning "true believers" against consorting with such persons or listening to their views, while appealing to the recalcitrant to mend their ways. One might mention that penal sanctions for infringements of the religious code, whenever enforceable, have tended to be rather inhuman, cruel and undignified.

Cult refers to the various rubrics that govern how official (individual or communitarian) worship of a particular religion is to be carried out. This may include a host of minutiae, such as who is authorised to conduct the form of prayer, what vestments the officiants are supposed to wear, what precise words and gestures are to be used when, which symbolic objects are to be employed in what way and at what precise moment in the vent, and so on. The degree of meticulousness with which these are to be observed avarice from religion to religion. Quite frequently it is required that the service be conducted in the same ancient language that was current when the religion first saw the light of day – even if the language is a dead one, a foreign tongue, In most cases, unknown to the vast majority of the devotees. Invariably the ritual is considered "invalid" and inefficacious if some item of these details has not been scrupulously observed.

h. Conclusion

It is these very concrete, very visible and obtrusive elements that most often irritate serious and sincere religious people. They want to encounter the divine in a community and express their devotion in words and gestures that rise spontaneously from themselves. But what happens when they enter a traditional place of worship? They are put into liturgical strait-jackets and told where they have to place themselves (far from the centre of activity), what passive roles they must play throughout (invariably, they are issued a handbook, with detailed instructions as to what pre-planned words and gestures they are permitted to use and at what moment). And, quite often, they are not permitted to address God in their own mother-tongue, the language of their hearts and most personal exchanges, but in some obscure discourse whose very alphabet (let alone meaning) is incomprehensible to them! As far rituals, few can figure out what they are all about – save a handful of erudite archaic specialists. So much for cult!

What of the elements of creed and code? Many a time these are couched in a form that has remained impervious to the development of science and technology. If people dare to voice their questions or doubts, they are often met with reproach and a call to practice the virtue of blind faith! It is these shameless bits of obscurantism, not to mention downright ignorance, that put off young people as well as religious seekers of a deeper, more personal conviction, driving them out of church, temple and other traditional places of worship.

This is borne out by the mushrooming of all manner of charismatic and "peoples' communities", where worship is more spontaneous and free, where leadership is shared by all the worshippers, who have a more active role to play, where clerical intervention is minimal, if not down to-absolute zero. It's not organised religion that is the real problem for most people, but the hierarchic, undemocratic and unspontaneous way it is organised!

"Everyday, people are straying away from the Church and going back toGod!" –Lenny Bruce (1925-1966)

"Men will wrangle for religion; write for it; fight for it; anything but live for it." –Charles Coulton (1780-1832)

"We have just enough religion to make us hate one another; we do not have quite enough religion to help us love one another." –Jonathan Swift (1667-1745)

Chapter 2

GOD AND/OR THE SACRED

a. Introductory Remarks

Most textbooks on the *Philosophy* of God tend to start with a discussion of proofs for the existence of God and, having dealt with that issue, proceed to talk about the essence of God (i.e. what does the term mean, what qualities or attributes are to be ascribed to the divinity?) However, my approach is just the opposite. I prefer to begin with a critical reflection on our understanding of God and thence take up the debate on whether God's existence can be proved or not. The reason is that I, with many others, am quite convinced that the reason why one believes in God or not depends on the concept of God one has previously formed in life. If that concept is meaningful and seen to be, not just no barrier to human growth and development, but a positive inspiration and support for it, he/she will believe in God, *and only then* cast about for "proofs" to justify his/her stance. Conversely, if a person has, in the light of his or her experiences and up – bringing, formed a negative concept of God (e.g. is convinced that belief in God necessarily degrades human dignity, responsibility and freedom), then such a person will become an atheist and, *as a result*, will assemble arguments against God's existence. Even if one were not to agree with my conviction, he might turn directly to my discussion of proofs for God's existence, which I take up in the next chapter.

b. God or the Sacred?

One naturally tends to think that the notion of God (though conceived differently) would be a kind of "least common denominator" in all religions.

But this is not quite true. There are at least two great religions that have existed for thousands of years and are quite capable of an atheistic interpretation; indeed, many of their adherents are "devout atheists" (however paradoxical to some of us that may seem). I am referring to Buddhism and Jainism, the latter being the religion that Gandhi was born into (he, of course, was a firm believer in God). But, if these systems are atheistic, why call them religions at all, one might, quite understandably ask? Well, for one thing, they – in common with other theistic religions – offer some kind of redemption or salvation from the human condition of ignorance, sin and suffering. They suggest ways and means to overcome our passions and attaining a depth of self-mastery and inner tranquillity. And isn't this part of the goals of all authentic religion. The most basic concept, common to all religions (including the atheistic variety) is the notion of the sacred. Some religious people interpret this is but a deeper, little-understood and lesser attained aspect of our own selves; others remain equally convinced that this is something totally new and unlike anything that we can experience in ourselves or the world around us, something that cannot be simply identified with any limited, finite thing of this world!

The Sacred: Durkheim & Co.

Emile Durkheim (1858-1917), a Frenchman who is considered the founding-father of "contemporary sociology, was a positivist, i.e., a philosopher of the nascent scientific age. Thus, he believed that only things that could be measured, weighed and counted, as in the field of the physical sciences, are real (*posita).*[4] He set himself the task of explaining religion and religious experiences in terms of *posita*. He popularised the distinction between things sacred and things profane and sought to isolate the "elementary forms of religious life"; in other words, just as a scientist establishes particular elements, molecules and atoms as the "building blocks" of the material world, he was quite convinced that, with a little effort, we would be able to separate out basic material units as the real elements of the so-called sacred which would then be shown up for what they were: nothing but material things wrongly invested with supernatural qualities. Falling back on the study of Melanesian tribal religious practices pioneered by R. H. Codrington, an English anthropologist, he proposed "*mana*" as the archaic source of the sacred. With Codrington, he believed that the totemism practised by the Melanesians was the most primitive expression of human religiosity and all our contemporary sophisticated religious practices and doctrines were no more than more complex elaborations of the same! In tribal worship, there emerged a strange, fearsome force (called *mana*) – especially in the frenzied ritual dancing around the totem pole – which accrued to the totem, symbol of the tribe or clan. It was believed by the natives that

4 *Posita* in Latin, would mean things that can be measured, the quantifiable!

somehow their tribal identity, tribal lore and tribal skill and courage in hunting and fighting accrued to the totem through the dancers and, at the same time, the accumulated wisdom and insights of their ancestors was transferred from there, through them, to the whole tribe. Totemic cult boils down to the cult of the clan and "the gods were the people conceived symbolically." Thus religion, God, the sacred, are nothing but useful ways to teach primitives how to be loyal to, and integrate themselves fully into, tribal society. Thus, having discovered the empirical identity of *mana*. Durkheim was quite convinced that he had shown convincingly enough that religion had no extra-worldly, supernatural grounds whatever.

Two contemporary scholars, both French and both Freudians, offer views along the same lines: *Laura Makarius* and *René Girard*, both of whom published their research in 1974. The former links her conclusions to issues linked to sex and general bias, the latter links his findings to the sublimation of our alleged instinct for violence.

Makarius traces the origin of the sacred to the sense of awe with which the primitive mind was accustomed to regard blood and the various taboos associated with it. The efficacity of *mana* (she uses the same word as Durkheim) stemmed from the ambivalence of blood: the fact that one who shed blood would experience its malefic effect which would render him impure; at the same time, however, some of its mysterious, ineffable and efficacious power would be also transmitted to the violator of the taboo. Makraius was sure that her theory would put to rest, once and for all, centuries of "pseudo – theological speculation" and enable us to see truly wherein the secret of religious experience really lay!

Girard suggests that the sacred is nothing but a disguised sublimation of our violent instinct. He adverts to the unabashedly violent element that is present in all religious worship – a victim is slaughtered, its blood is spilt on the altar and sprinkled on the worshippers (albeit in an "unbloody" manner in some circle! The "scapegoat theory" (i.e. an innocent creature is cruelly slain to expiate the sins of the community by taking them on itself) is rejected by him. Rather, it is a "surrogate victim" (*une victime emissaire*), which thereby absorbs the violence that men (!), prey to their drive, would otherwise be driven to vent on each other. His thesis, he sees, is confirmed by his claim that "sacrifice languished in societies with a firmly established judicial system – ancient Greece and Rome, for example." How that we have an efficient legal system and a well-trained police force to enforce it, we no longer require the sublimatory effects of religion to control our violent drives.

c. The Sacred: Soderblom & Co.

Nathan Söderblom (1866-1931) was a Swede, one of the pioneers in the study Comparative Religions, at his native University of Upsala. He wrote a very significant article, "Holiness" for the *Encyclopaedia of Religion and Ethics*, which proved to be a landmark in the development of the Philosophy of Religion. "The sacred is the most important word in religion; it is even more so than God", he tellingly remarked. He then went on to say why: "For a religion can really exist without any conception of the divinity, but there is no real religion without the distinction between the sacred and the profane." Next, he provides us with a kind of descriptive definition of the sacred: it is "a power or entity, mysterious, and bound up with certain things, events or actions." Finally, he sub-divided the sacred into two constitutive parts, one with a more positive connotation, *mana*, a beneficial efficacious power and another with a more negative connotation, *taboo*, "implying the notion of danger, of interdict and prohibition." Söderblom was an orthodox Christian and rejected any interpretation of the sacred as an impersonal force, a deeper and most often untapped resource of the individual or society. For him an encounter with the sacred stemmed from a genuine contact with God. He concluded that all would agree that "the psychological origin of the concept of the sacred seems to have been the reaction of the mind when confronted with something which is new, stalling and terrifying." Since then, most scholars use the term *ganz Andere* as a kind of synonym for the Sacred.

Rudolf Otto (1869-1937), the German savant and mystic, was impressed with the work of Söderblom and set out on his studies with the last quoted phrase of the latter ringing in his ears. A profoundly religious man himself, he avowed he was a "Lutheran Benedictine" and made no secret of his love for the beauty and solemnity of the Roman Catholic liturgy, together with its scope for facilitating an encounter with the divine. But he devoted himself with equal zeal to the study of non-Christian religions as to Christian theology. A visit to India convinced him that the Sacred can be encountered more fully through intuition and symbol and far less adequately through reason. His Indian experience, coupled with his delving into the Upanishads, convinced Otto of the greatness and completeness of Indian mysticism. He was further gratified to discover a tremendous convergence in the mystics of Europe, India, Israel, Iran, China and Greece.

But behind the wealth of ideas and practices that he documented in religions across the globe, there seemed to loom one common and incontestable phenomenon, the sense of the Holy. In practice, however, *das Heilige* was also used in Ethics and was applied to certain human beings. In search of a more precise and specialised term that could be exclusively used for the encounter with the divine in religion, he decided to leave the "holy" to Ethics and coin a new term for religious language: "(The Latin) *omen* has given us 'ominous' and there is no reason why from *numen*[5] should not from, similarly, a word, 'numinous'."

He then sifts through piles of writings of mystics of every race and age and creed to summarise these into four phenomenological steps in the human encounter with the numinous. First, there is elicited from us a "creaurely feeling" (*das Kreaturgefuhl*). Here is an expression of "the emotion of a creature, submerged and overwhelmed by its own nothingness in contrast to that which is supreme above all creatures." Then comes the stage of the *tremendum*, holy fear and mystic awe, which makes one tend to draw back in the face of the mystery of the All-Good and the All-Pure. This is practically simultaneous with a kind of contrary movement, which he uses two Greek words, to describe, *eusebeia* or *eulabela*, an overwhelming urge from deep within to express one's feelings through deep piety and cultic acts. Any authentic cultic rite, Otto unceasingly reminds us, must issue forth in a powerful confession of the Mystery, the Wholly Other, the Totally Transcendent. This, culminates in the final experience of the *fascinans*, the fascinating – that which seduces, enraptures and draws human into bliss.

Mircea Eliade (1907-1986), the celebrated Rumanian scholar of religions, arrived in India in 1928, studied at Calcutta and produced a brilliant doctoral thesis on *yoga*. When his country turned Communist after World War II, he assumed voluntary exile, relinquishing his governmental post and settling down in France. From Paris, he launched a series of books, articles and conferences on the History of Religions. Later, he shifted to the United States and was attached to the University of Chicago. He agrees that the Sacred is the basis of all religious experience and observes, "Man becomes aware of the sacred, because it manifests itself as something quite different from the profane." He coins the term *hierophany* to describe this manifestation of the Sacred. It is significant, he notes, that a *hierophany* always occurs through the medium of "myths or symbols, but never completely in an immediate manner in its totality." In other words, the infinite humbly historicises itself in and through some finite reality. "This is the great mystery, the *mvsterum tremendum,*" he avers, "the fact that the Sacred decided to limit Itself" in a *hierophany*!

In Response to Durkheim & Co

Durkheim's reductionist approach would hardly stand up to contemporary views. Understandably was he so enamoured by the positive sciences as they were just coming into being. Postmodernism would make short shrift to erstwhile claims to found epistemological certainties on the findings of science.' Even contemporary philosophers of science, from Capra to Einstein and Heisenberg are wary about any claims to absolutism and naive objectivity

5 Latin for 'divinity!

that are associated with nineteenth century positivism. Besides, as further anthropological and sociological studies have shown, it is far- too simplistic a thesis to hold that all religion is nothing more than souped-up totem dancing!

As for Makarius and Girard, they have certainly made some insightful comments on the phenomenon of religious rites, but can we afford to receive them without serious critical thought? Again, it is sociologists, like Evans-Pritchard who caution us against any hasty tendency to study or explain away one discipline from the perspective of, or in terms of, another. It is not scientific to rule out a *priori* the reality of any discipline's subject-matter and then proceed to study biology as if it were engineering or vice versa!

More to the point, the American thinker and psychologist, William James (1842-1910) had this to say about people *who try to "show up" religion as* perverted sexuality or sublimated violence:

> It is true that in the vast collection of religious phenomena, some are undisguisedly amatory – e.g., sex deities and obscene rites in polytheism and ecstatic feelings of union with the Saviour in a few Christian "mystics. But then,' why not call religion an aberration of the digestive function and prove one's point by the worship of Bacchus and Ceres, or the ecstatic feelings of some saints about the Eucharist? Religious language clothes itself in such poor symbols as life affords, and the whole organism gives overtones of comment whenever the mind is strongly stirred to expression. Language drawn from eating and drinking is probably as common in religious literature as is language drawn from sexual life.

The quote is from his classic, *The Varieties of Religious Experience.*[6] Now, danger of all reductionisms is that they fasten themselves upon a point which may be true, but thence proceed to the simplistic generalisation that all instances of anything linked with the fact are to be explained in the same way. This is the traditional fallacy of arguing, "That convicted murderer has red hair, therefore all red-haired people are prone to commit murder!" Trying to maintain that *all* religious activity can be explained away as sex and violence would force one to conclude, with equal (il) logic that

> ...: the religious life depends just as much upon the spleen, the pancreas and on the kidneys as on the sexual apparatus, and the whole theory has (by now) lost its point in evaporating into a vague general assertion off the dependence, *somehow*, of the mind upon the body.

And no one would quarrel with that last remark – except to note that it is so vague and general as to practically say nothing worth paying attention to!

---

6 James, William. *The Varieties of Religious Experience: A Study in Human Nature, Being the Gifford Lectures on Natural Religion Delivered at Edinburgh in 1901-1902, by William James*. New York, London: Longmans, Green, and Co, 1902.

d. Popular Idols of God

An idol is a man-made, humanly fabricated thing which is, consciously or not, taken to be God. Nor should we imagine that idolatry is a curious bit of religious archaeology and that nobody in these enlightened times goes in for that sort of thing nowadays, thank you! Quite apart from many cultural idols worshipped by some of our contemporaries – money, sex and the State to mention Just a few, there are not a few bona fide religious people who scarce seem to realise that the "God" they are worshipping, praying to and reverencing is a false god, a figment of their imagination, a "plastic divinity" that enables them to practice their favourite follies, vices and uncommited-ness without any disturbance. Such "gods" are easy to get along with, tailored, as they are, to our own specifications, there is no danger of them shaking us out of our accustomed, inactive slumber. Voltaire has said it most aptly, "God made man in his own image and likeness and man returned the compliment." This kind of religious idolatry is seldom done with "full knowledge and full consent"; indeed, it is mostly done unconsciously. Such deviant and misleading practices must be shown up for what they are so that we can get on with the real job of seeking to know God in all authenticity.

a. The "aspirin" god: This god functions like our preferred anti-headache pill. Such analgesics (the contemporary "opium of the people") are an indispensable part of everyone's medicine cabinet. It is good policy to keep a few of such "soothers" handy: who knows when the next migraine or hangover will present itself? In which case, all we have to do is dose ourselves with the appropriate tablets ... and promptly forget about them until the next headache! Now, the "god" of many would-be religious people is just like that.' He exists, all right (just as one's "aspirin" does), within reach and one believes In His efficacious power (just like those wonderful pills). But such people only relate to their "god" when they've some kind of a spiritual "headache"; one's the crisis is over he's forgotten. Of course, we *should* turn to God, as to a reliable friend, for strength, support and inspiration at harrowing times – but assuredly not *only* at such times, demanding immediate solutions at our own terms, or else... Could this be one of the reasons why, for many people, their prayer-life remains so shallow and stagnant? Doesn't the "prayer " of such people boil down to nothing more than a "shopping list for a super-market god"? And, when such people find that they are not rendered prompt and efficient service, don't they threaten to boycott the store?

b. The "puppeteer" god : This is the deity worshipped by all who have a naive understanding of Divine Providence. They reduce phrases like "God's will" to the predetermination of our lives down to the last detail. In effect, all that happens in this world is the result of a cleverly-staged puppet show, with "god" pulling all the strings. This kind of believer does even manage to derive some kind of comfort from this kind of god in times of crisis. "Well, God knows best", they say. "He made this happen and so it must be for our overall good !" There is no doubt that they even gain some sort of peace of mind in the face of adversity, through this act of pious resignation. But the price they have to pay for this simplistic solution is an abdication of a good deal of responsibility and active initiative in the world. Besides, all this expert puppetry ends up laying the blame of gang-rape, child abuse and the attempted genocide of Hitler's Nazis (to mention just a few unsavoury things) at the door of the string-puller. Most religions are committed to both human freedom and divine providence. It is foolish polity (to say the very least) to claim to uphold both in one forum and then blithely proceed to sacrifice one to save the other in a different context!

c. The "policeman" god : This is the "god" of those people whose only reason for not running riot, bullying the weak and terrorising the powerless is that Big Brother is watching them, keeping a meticulous record of all their doings on planet earth so that He can dish out to them so many hours of penal servitude here or hereafter to make up for their sundry little peccadilloes. But isn't this representative of a rather retarded moral consciousness? Surely a mature adult should be able to find something better than a "carrot-and-stick" approach to restrain him from rape and mayhem? Can't he recognise that there's something inherently repulsive in forcibly deflowering a hapless maiden – can't he recognise the utterly dishonorable nature of the deed: how it dehumanises both the victim and the aggressor? After all, lollipops and beatings may be OK enough when one is trying to get an immature child to study, but it would be laughable (and worse!) to come across a grown-up allegedly mature adult who wants the equivalent of a lollipop each time he does his duty, or who needs the threat of punishment to make him behave!

d. Some other "gods": One "could prolong the list of such idols. There is the *laundromat "god"*, one used by the believer to get his soul "purified" of sin quite easily, at routine intervals (confession or a dip in the holy river)... and so one takes moral obligation rather casually. After all, one doesn't get too upset about soiling his nice white shirt because a trip to the corner laundromat will get it back good as new-in a jiffy. In a similar manner, the shallow believer nurtures a rather cavalier attitude towards moral behaviour: no need to be over scrupulous about faults of various natures: ones "laundromat god" will clean up his soul in a trice, at no great cost to time or money or energy! Then there's the *racist "god"*, the one that assures me that only I, and those few others whose religious views happen to coincide with mine, would be "saved"; the rest, a veritable "*massa damnata*" are to be consigned to eternal perdition, no matter how moral or blameless their lives might be. This pernicious view arises from a misunderstanding of scriptural assurances that one is part of a "chosen people". A closer perusal of the relevant texts, however, would make it clear that "divine choice" doesn't at all imply a rejection of the rest! In fact, such "choice", far from allocating to the "elect" privileges denied to others, merely shoulders them with the heavy responsibility of proclaiming God's unconditional love for all people, irrespective of race, sex or creed!

e. The "Masters of Suspicion"

It was Paul Ricoeur, the devout Christian French phenomenologist, who dubbed the atheist trio Nietzsche-Marx-Freud, "Masters of Suspicion", since they, in effect, have taught us to be suspicious of hastily assuming that we have had mystical experiences: often times, they point out, what we were really encountering was nothing divine or supernatural but some little understood and unhealthy aspect of ourselves. J. P. Stern, in his deceptively slim, masterful work on Nietzsche[7] summed up their perennial critique of religion:

> They saw their undertaking as the solving of a secret, and all opposition to it as a conspiracy; a conspiracy of men with vested social interests, thought Marx; of men with vested moral and religious interests, thought Freud; of men who chose to be only half alive and resent the few who live generously and dangerously, thought Nietzsche.

a. Karl Marx (1816-1883): According to the father of all leftists, "Religion is the opium of the people." This is one of the world's most famous quotations. What is *not* so well known, however, is that he held that it was the oppressed people who dose themselves with opium (a pain-killer in Marl's days) to deaden the pain of their sufferings. It was not the oppressors who gave it to them to make them keep quiet! Now, there's nothing wrong with making use of a pain-killer *when there is no way of removing the source* of *one's pain* (as in some cases of cancer, or in a post-operation situation)? But if one has, say, a thorn in the foot, the proper remedy would he to remove the thorn, not leave it there and take pain-killers. Marx is quite right in attacking all those victims of social injustice who, instead of rising up to challenge their oppressor and demand their just rights, resign themselves to their lot and look for "pie in the sky when they die". And when such is the case, we cannot hut endorse Marx's critique and do all we can to extirpate such pseudo-religiosity, conscientising the people to put forward concerted action for justice! However, not all religion functions as an opium, nor are believers miserable and oppressed people. Authentic religion, far from being the opium of the people, can be a catalyst for revolutionary action for justice, as the activists of liberation theology (and philosophy!) show.

b. Friederich Nietzsche (1844-1901): Granted, Nietzsche ended his days in an asylum for the insane; granted, many of his strident rantings against God and religion appear to warrant no more attention than we'd give to the babblings

7 Stern, J P. *A Study of Nietzsche.* Cambridge: Cambridge University Press, 1981.

of any madman. But, behind and the apparent arrogance and decidedly schizophrenic utterances, there is a solid vein of critical truth that we would be foolish and irresponsible to ignore. His charge is that religion in general, and Christianity in particular, has proved for a good many people a pious subterfuge for cowardice and mediocrity, masquerading under the "virtues" of humility and resignation to Sod! For too long have religions frowned upon ambition, self-assertion and courageous initiative, over-stressing counterfeits for meekness and gentleness. Nietzsche does well to remind us that the former have a positive side and the latter hide a negative aspect. On the other hand, a disproportionate emphasis on "the "manly" virtues, without situating them in their proper humanising context, can lead to the worst excesses of colonialism, oppression … and Hitlerism.

c. Sigmund Freud (1856-1939): If Marx qualified religion as an opium, for Freud it was an *Illusion.* By this he didn't mean that it was patently false – in which case he would have qualified it as *delusion.* What the Austrian father of psycho-analysis meant was that "wish-fulfillment", more than anything else was its basis. As an illustration of what he meant by this, he asked us to consider the case of a servant girl, who is badly treated by the family for which she works. She could protest and throw up her job, but instead she carries on her miserable drudgery, hoping all along that a handsome prince will one day come along, marry her and rescue her from her pitiful state, taking her to live happily ever after with him in a glorious castle. Now, handsome princes do exist and it is at least theoretically possible that one of them just might come her way, fall in love with her and take her with him to his fairy palace. But it is highly unlikely and she is pinning her hopes on an idle dream. People in misery fashion for themselves an illusory being called God, who, they hope will one day set them free from their suffering and take them off to heaven! Again, Freud compared religious believers to adults who are afraid to grow up and accept the responsibility for their own lives and futures. Realising that they cannot always be running to their earthly fathers for protection and for solutions to their problems (their earthly fathers die or are discovered by them, to their horror, *not* to be the strongest and most knowledgeable people on earth), they project their frustration into a "heavenly father" to whom they can run with all their problems and fears. Now, here too we must admit that there is a good deal of truth in what Freud has said: for many people "god" is nothing but wish-fulfilment and a projection of the father image – very specially for the psychologically disturbed people who came to him for counselling and healing. But Freud's mistake was his' over-generalisation: not everyone who believes in God or practices religious worship is psychotic! Henri Bergson (1859-1941), the French thinker and scholar on evolution, joining his research to that of William James (whom we have referred to above) has pointed out that in every culture and in every age there have been – and continue to be –

great mystics, people of all ages and sexes, who claim to have encountered God. Now it is possible to study their lives and writings and dismiss many of them as cranks, social misfits, psychologically deranged people who had – consciously or not – fabricated such "mystical experiences" out of their own inadequacies, insecurities and fears, seeking thereby a kind of escapist solution to their worries and anxieties. But we can't write off with equal ease all the claims of all mystics everywhere and at all time. Some of them, when critically examined, emerge as personages of obvious and evident psychological maturity and balance, radical thinkers who challenged the existing social and Religious structures of their times and were frequently persecuted and pilloried by the powers that were at the time both sacred and secular! They evince the qualities of gifted administrators, inspiring leaders , launching revolutionary movements and gathering around themselves charismatic and radical personalities who have helped to keep alive, even to our times, some of the action groups that they built up, These are hardly qualities we'd associate with "crazies"; instead, they stand out as psychologically sound as the best of us, if not more so! Thus not all mystics and their writings would wilt and pale before the ruthless assault of philosophical "suspicion"!

"If God did not exist, it would be necessary to invent him!"
–Voltaire

"She god of the cannibals will be a cannibal, of the crusaders a crusader, and of the merchants a merchant." –Emerson

"Men show no mercy and expect no mercy, when honour calls, or when they fight for their idols or their gods." –Schiller

Chapter 3

FOR AND AGAINST GOD'S EXISTENCE

1. Introductory Ideas

a. Avoiding Extremes

We have already seen how it would be counter-productive in the long run (and not very helpful in the short run, either) to advocate the extreme approaches of either "blind faith" (fideism) or "pure reason" (exaggerated rationalism) in matters religious. Thence, we came to the conclusion that something of a "middle way", between the two would be most appropriate and we have described that as the path of "reasonable risk". In other words, in establishing God's existence (as in any ascertaining the authenticity of any interpersonal relationship) we can expect to do no better than indicate sufficient grounds for taking a reasonable risk that what we believe in is real and true and not just a figment of our imagination and pure wishful thinking. There is *some* evidence, yes; but it is not absolutely conclusive "beyond-any-shadow-of-doubt" evidence. Furthermore, we added, if one were to say that he couldn't "buy" such a way of proceeding then, by that same token, to be consistent one will have to reject also every possibility of falling in love or having a friend: only "reasonable risk" can justify those interpersonal commitments! All commitments presuppose faith and all faith is based on reasonable risk.

b. Belief that and Belief in

That last remark necessitates my bringing in the famous distinction between belief *in* and belief *that* which, as we shall see, helps throw a lot of light on the relationship between faith and reason. Though in common, everyday speech we use the two phrases as if they had the same connotations yet, philosophically speaking, perhaps it would be helpful to distinguish carefully between their implications. Take the statement, "I believe that the Taj Mahal exists." The fact that I say, "I believe..." in this case, and not "I *know*.. seems to indicate that I've not seen or visited the Taj Mahal myself: I know of its existence indirectly, through reports of trustworthy people who've been there or from photographs or videos and films. In fact, that is precisely the connotation of, "I believe *that* ..." A "belief that" is a matter of accepting that such-and-such is the case or that, someone exists (e.g. "I believe that Elisabeth II is the Queen of England."). But a "belief in..." expresses much more (e.g. I say to a friend, "I believe in you!"): trust, personal commitment, love – all of which are missing in a strict "belief that". Strictly speaking, if we reflect on it a bit, we can only speak of belief in with regard to people whom we love. When people ask us questions like, "Do you believe in God/the devil/ghosts?" what they actually mean is, "Do you believe *that* God/the devil/ghosts exist?"

c. Proofs and Belief that

Now, a rational proof for God's existence (whatever be its validity) – like a rational proof for anything's existence – can only give us "belief that", never "belief in". That is to say, rational proofs can, at best, convince us that such and such is the case or that something or someone exists. It can never lead us to trust in, or love someone. A valid proof for God's existence might elicit from someone a remark like, OK. So this 'God' you talk so much about exists. Fine. So does the Taj Mahal. Both don't move me to action or have any impact on my life!" It's not enough to "believe that" God exists. Authentic religion begins where belief that leaves off: authentic religion is founded on trust in God, love of God ... belief ... and rational proofs cannot give us that.

This is not to say that rational proofs have no" use or value at all in religion and faith. They help deepen one's convictions and, in their absence, one's faith would be easily shaken (if not lost) in moments of adversity or doubt (and this is part of all human life). Besides rational proofs (based on reasonable risk, don't forget!) would show to another that my faith in God has some basis and is not a kind of infantile blind belief, like a child's faith in fairies or Santa Claus.

d. Hermeneutics

Hermeneutics is a fairly new word for something that we've all been doing, though not very consciously. Hermeneutics traces its etymology to the Greek god Hermes (recognisable by his winged-ankles and dynamic pose!), who was supposed to have taught humans how to speak. Significantly enough, he was also the god of lies and deceit. This implies an ancient insight into the fact that language can be equally used to falsely conceal, or truthfully reveal, our thoughts and dispositions. Hence arises the need to interpret and, for practical purposes, we might define hermeneutics, at this stage, as the science and art of hermeneutics. We "do hermeneutics" several times a day: when we read a letter, scan the newspapers or engage in conversation or study someone's "body language". It is not only done by theologians when they busy themselves with scripture study and interpretation, or with students of literature when they try to figure out what a poet or dramatist was trying to "say" through his/her creative work.

What I want to stress at this point is that much of our so-called "rational proofs" (whether they concern God's existence, life after death, or whether X is really in love, with me or not) are not so much "rational proofs" but interpretations of what we observe. Thus, for instance, the atheist and the theist both live in the same world and are confronted with the same factual data. Their difference of conviction arises from how they interpret the same facts. Both, for instance, see and note the horrifying fact of injustice, evil and the suffering of the innocent (side by side with the prospering of the corrupt!). The atheist interprets this fact as a "proof" that God doesn't exist: "I can't believe in a God who would allow innocent children to suffer!" declared French existentialist, Albert Camus (1913-1961). The theist re-interprets the same fact in another way, say, in the light of the Cross, if he/she is a Christian: "Suffering is our sharing in God's struggle to liberate the world", as contemporary liberation thinker Gustavo Guttierez would say.

e. Summing up

Before we pass on to reviewing the more well-known arguments for and against God's existence, let us sum up the main points I have tried to make so far.

First, I would say that there is no cogent, decisive and conclusive evidence in favour of either theism or atheism; there is sufficient data, however, *to make a reasonably good case either way!* Secondly, hermeneutics, rather than rational proofs is the ultimate deciding factor. And, thirdly, rational proofs are useful up to a point. They help to confirm my already established conviction that God exists (based, as I have tried to show, on my having constructed for myself, out of my experiences, a meaningful understanding of God's existence). They further enable me to show to an agnostic that my faith in God is, at least, reasonable – unlike a child's naive belief in the tooth fairy, say. But, any proof propose, however valid – has its limitations. At best it can lead one to mere "belief that" and never to "belief in". And, in the last analysis, it is "belief in" that ultimately matters in religion. With all these provisos, we now take up the (rational) grounds for and against belief in God. After that we will have something to say about leading a person from belief that to belief in.

2. Arguments for God's Existence

a. The Ontological Argument

History: This daft bit of reasoning was first proposed by Anselm of Canterbury (1033-1109), later canonised by the Catholic Church. He presented it in his famous *Prologion* (chapters 2-4).[8] It was taken up by Descartes and Leibniz (seventeenth century rationalists), with a few modifications. It was Kant (1724-1804) who nick-named it the "ontological" argument, because it started from a certain way of conceiving the notion of being. Like the pious bishop that he was, Anselm began his "proof" with a quotation from the Bible, the Book of Psalms. To be precise "The fool has said in his heart, 'There is no God.'" (14:1). He then proceeds to show why the psalmist is justified, in calling the atheist a fool. His reasoning is that an atheist is a fool because he contradicts himself when he denies God's existence: he contradicts himself because the very fact that he is able to form the concept of God obliges him to grant God's existence. In other words, the very concept of God implies God's existence.

Formulation: The atheist, when he denies God's existence, surely knows what is meant by the word, "God" – if he doesn't even know what it means, how could he assert that no reality corresponding to it existed? So, he grants the concept of God, at least. Now, what does this concept mean? Surely "a being than which nothing greater can be thought". Once the atheist agrees with this definition (which is just about what every dictionary gives as the meaning of the word, viz., "supreme being", "infinite being" etc), then, according to Anselm, he is "had"! For such a being would have to exist: if it did not, then it wouldn't be the "being than which nothing greater can exist", for anything that exists – even a speck of dust – would be greater than God, for inasmuch as it existed it would be superior to God, who did not exist! Putting it in a slightly different fashion, one could say that, by God, is meant a being who has all perfections. But this would mean that God must have existence, as existence is also a perfection. Thus, once you grant the concept of God, you are obliged to grant his existence!

Objections: One of the first to leap into the fray was Gaunilo, a monk of Marmoutiers in France and Anselm's contemporary, who felt that the English was giving the atheist a raw deal. In his *On Behalf of the Fool*,[9] he argued that were we to accept the *Proslogion* proof, all manner of absurdities would follow for, in the same way, the mere fact that one could form the concept of

8 Anselm, Sidney N. Deane, Anselm, Gaunilo, and Anselm. *St. Anselm: Proslogium ; Monologium ; an Appendix in Behalf of the Fool by Gaunilon ; and Cur Deus Homo*. La Salle, Ill: Open Court Pub, 1958.

9 Gaunilo, and A. *Gaunilo, in Behalf of the Fool, and Anselm, Reply*. New York, N.Y: Internet History Sourcebooks Project, 2000.

a most perfect island (or, to use a more modern example, that of a stairway to the stars), we would have to grant their existence? But Anselm retorted – and rightly! – that Gaunilo had missed the point. Only the concept of a most perfect being (i.e. one that is perfect from the aspect of being, that is, all-round perfect) implies its existence. The most perfect island concept is most perfect from the aspect of island only, not being. So the absurdities do not follow. And, as we have said, Anselm was right! It was left to Immanuel Kant to point out the real flaw in Anselm's argument. Bertrand Russel (1872-1970) would repeat and develop the same objection in the light of his personal views. It boils down to the fact that Anselm has erroneously treated "existence" as if it were part of "what a being is" (its essence). Now a concept tells us precisely what something is, therefore it contains only its "whatness". But existence is not something like that. It doesn't add to what a thing is: rather it tells us that a thing is. Hence, the concept of anything (even of the most perfect being) does not – cannot – pre-contain its existence!

Conclusion: This "proof" doesn't really hold water. At most it is a help to a better understanding of God. Such is the view of the Swiss Protestant theologian, Karl Barth (1886-1968).

b. The Cosmological Arguments

History: There are more than two attempts to prove God's existence, starting with some observed aspect of the world (Greek, *kosmos*). Their most forceful presentation is the version of Thomas Aquinas (1224-1275), an Italian monk who was also canonised later. They are to be found among his celebrated "five ways to prove God's existence" (*quinaue viae*) in his epochal *Summa Theologiae* (Summary of Theology). I, 2, 3. He did not invent any of these "ways": they had already been used by Aristotle, Plato and others before him. One or more of these arguments, indeed, are to be found in just about every nation and culture, since classical times. Aquinas' merit was in the way he marshalled them into form. They all take, as their major premise (to use the terminology of Aristotelian logic, which they fall back upon) some form of the famous "principle of causality". The minor premises are some, observed fact in the world.

Then, after rejecting "infinite regress" they arrive at the existence of God who is discovered under the name most appropriately following from the thrust of the argument. The important difference between Aquinas' approach, as contrasted with Anselm's is that the former starts with some concrete observed data, taken from the actual world, and not a concept, as in Anselm's method!

Formulation: Here we will consider only the first, second and third ways.

Form 1: Whatever moves or changes is moved by another. This is the "major" premise of the argument (NOTE: In Latin, *movetur* refer to change in general, not just "local change" or movements hence we use both words in translation). Now, it is certain that in this world, at least some' things do change. But there can't be an endless regress of changing things and changers. Hence there must be some first unchanged changer (Latin, *motor immobilis*) which could also be translated as "unmoved mover". And this is but another name for God.

Form 2: Whatever happens in the world requires a cause. This is the major premise. An alternative form of, the "principle of causality" as was expressed above. Now it is certain that some things do happen in this world and there cannot be an infinite regress of causes which, in turn, were caused by other causes. Hence there must be a first uncaused cause to start the whole process. And this is but another name for God.

Form 3: Contingent beings presuppose a necessary being. This is a third variation of the "principle of causality". As regards the terminology a "contingent" being is a being which exists but doesn't have to exist; a "necessary" being is one which exists and cannot not-exist. The "minor", as is to be expected asserts that "it is certain that there are contingent beings in this world" and cites "generation and corruption" as indications of this (viz. the fact of things coming into being and, after some time, perishing). Hence, there must be some first neccesary being, to get the process going.

Objections: In the first place, all these "proofs" assume the validity of the "famous principle of causality" – something which everybody in Aquinas' time was quite ready to grant. But, David Hume (1711-1776), the Scottish empiricist, who vaunted his universal scepticism, quite satisfyingly showed that it cannot simply be "taken for granted" (the details of his critique are too complicated to go into, in detail, here). Thus, the "major premise" or foundation of the whole argument collapses. Furthermore, the ruling out of infinite regress is not so straightaway justifiable – as even Aquinas noted (cf. later in his same work, Question 63, article 2) for it boils down to saying that if we refuse to reject it, then the world would be a "mere unintelligible brute fact" – but this is precisely what the sceptic holds!

c. The Teleological Argument

History: This is the argument found in most popular text-books, as it is quite easy to understand and appears to base itself on scientific discovery. Plato uses it in his *Timaeus*[10] and Aquinas presents it as his "fifth way". The scientist-philosopher Kant, though he had his reservations about it, felt constrained to

10 Plato and Oskar Piest. *Timaeus*. New York: Liberal Arts Press, 1959.

hail it as "the oldest, the clearest and the most accordant with the common reason of mankind."

Formulation: Order requires a wise orderer. This "major" is, once again, a re-statement of the "principle of causality". It is based on the presupposition that mere chance can't explain order and regularity. The "minor" points out to the fact that there is a natural order in the world – the various "laws of nature" that science is ever discovering, both at the microscopic and the macroscopic level. Hence, the conclusion: there must be an ultimate wise orderer and that is what we mean by God.

Objection: Apart from the fact that this argument also hangs from the shaky nails of the "principle of causality", there are other difficulties. As Hume, himself, observed, it is inevitable that the universe appear to be the result of intelligent design. But the fact of accommodation and adaptation, on which evolution is based, can afford us another explanation for order. As John Hick, the Anglican priest and thinker remarks,

> To refer back to the **ozone** layer, the reason animal life on earth is so marvellously sheltered by this filtering arrangement is not that God created the animals first and then put the ozone layer in place to protect them, but rather the **ozone** layer was there first, and only those forms of life capable of existing in the precise level of ultra-violet radiation that penetrates this layer have developed on earth.

d. The Moral Argument

History: Among its more well-known exponents may be ranked Immanuel Kant – as also the English Anglican clergyman who later became a Catholic, a Cardinal and whose cause is currently being discussed for canonisation, John Henry Newman (1801-1890).[11] The tone of his argument is more representative of the various versions of it that we come across in contemporary religious apologetic. Here is a relevant extract from his monumental *Grammar of Assent*:[12]

> If, as is the case, we feel responsibility, are ashamed, are frightened, at the transgressing the voice of conscience, this implies that there is One to whom we are responsible, before whom we are ashamed, whose claims upon us we fear. … If the cause of these emotions do not belong to this visible world, the Object to which [the conscientious person's] perception is directed must be Supernatural and Divine.

---

11 Please note that he will be canonised on October 13, 2019.

12 Newman, John Henry, *An Essay in Aid of a Grammar of Assent*. New York, N.Y. : Chelsea House, 2014.

Objections: Among these, the most significant is the suggestion that there may be alternative explanations for the "voice of conscience", namely human needs, self-interest and society. One cannot rule these out a priori: that would be begging the question. On the other hand, it could be pointed out that, as many of us have observed, the "inner voice" very often goes against these very alternatives, so can't be so simplistically identified with them. Sociologists and psychologists of an agnostic or atheistic stance would not be convinced by this rejoinder and the discussion would then move onto intricate aspects of depth psychology and the unconscious.

e. The Religious Experience Argument

History: The most forceful presentation of this approach is that of Bergson or James, to whom I have alluded, above. A more recent case is that of André Frossard, a former agnostic who, in his *God Exists: I've Met Him* tells how this French journalist, working for Figaro experienced a sudden conversion to Catholicism, the decisive moment in this being a strange, irresistible urge that he felt to enter a quiet chapel as he was passing by. There is also the story of the erstwhile persecutor of Christians, Saul, who, after his "Damascus experience" became an ardent Christian apostle and missionary!

Objections: One cannot discount the power of such experiences for those who have had them; the problem is trying to convince one who has not had such an experience. David Hume, in his essay on "Miracles"[13] notes that one could either deny outright the veracity of such reports or attempt alternative explanations, such as telepathy, hallucinations and the like. Thomas Hobbes (1588-1679), the English thinker and agnostic remarked, tongue in cheek, that a man who says that God spoke to him in a dream is but a man who has dreamt! Bergson and James, we have seen, assert that the "great chorus of witnesses" cannot be so easily written off. A good many of them, as was mentioned, can be shown to be people of great moral worth (hence, whose veracity can't be very reasonably questioned); and the general thrust of their very active lives would render charges of hallucination and so on very unlikely. Still, the dissenter might end up saying that until a similar experience happened to him/her, he/she would withhold any religious belief or commitment!

f. The Greater Probability Argument

History: This is the approach favoured by many contemporary philosophers of religion. The approach is to take off from a combination of factors, a wider range of data than the exclusively teleological or moral and conclude that a theistic or religious worldview is the most reasonable explanation of

13 Cf Hume, David. *Enquiry Concerning Human Understanding, an*. South Bend: Infomotions, Inc, 2000.

all these facts. Such a view was espoused by F R Tennant in his two volume opus, *Philosophical Theology.*[14] Since then many others have emulated and improved upon his method.

Formulation: A very wide range of relevant data is collected and serves as the starting point for this approach – the teleological character of biological evolution as also the whole wealth of human religious, moral, aesthetic and cognitive experience. An effort is made to show how each of these, independently, seems to be pointing towards a supernatural source. Even if one were to say that each separate "pointer" is no conclusive enough, surely the accumulated evidence of each pointing individually towards the same point would suggest, that belief in God would be the most probable worldview wherein to find a satisfactory explanation of the listed phenomena. All this is very true but it cannot be denied that the religious conviction that one has sought to vindicate by this approach is based on "greater probability" (or "reasonable risk"!) But, by that same token, one would have to admit that an atheistic stance is also a viable "reasonable risk" or, at least in the dissenter's view, perhaps as probable an explanation!

3. Arguments Against God's Existence

a. The Sociological Objection

History: We've already had occasion to speak of Emile Durkheim who, in his *Elementary Forms of Religious Experience* (1912)[15] both typfies, and is the best argued example of, the views of his school of nascent Sociology.

Formulation: To briefly review what has been outlined above, held that all religion is nothing more than a disguised from of social control, the gods were the "people considered symbolically" and all this was supposed to be borne out by totemism, which he saw as the most basic and elementary form of religious practice. Others, following in his footsteps, updated, here and there, some of his insights but generally kept the basic thrust of his argument.

Objections: Once again, we review the main points made above. First, it is difficult to explain how the universal reach of a religiously formed conscience could transcend the boundaries of a closed tribal group and attain anything like the universal love of the more open religious community. Nor is it possible to explain how the moral creativity of the prophetic mind developed: how could they have found, once again, within the confines of closed tribal society the insight to make such far-reaching claims on our ethical life? Nor can we

14 Tennant, Frederick R. *Philosophical Theology: (in Two Volumes)*. Cambridge: University Press, 1928.

15 Durkheim, Emile, and Anthony Giddens. *Emile Durkheim: Selected Writings*. West Nyack: Cambridge University Press, 1972.

account for the socially detaching power of their conscience. For prophetic figures have often gone against the norms of their society and were persecuted by it for that reason. How do we explain this, if we want to explain God as the same society in disguise?

Conclusion: The sociological theory doesn't conclusively prove that there is no God!

b. The Psychological Objection

History: We've already had occasion to discuss this, too. Freud had sought to "show" that the whole idea of God and religion is nothing but a kind of mental defence against threats, real or imagined. He dismissed religious beliefs as "illusions, fulfillments of the oldest, strongest and most insistent wishes of mankind." We have also outlined the objections developed by two of his more recent disciples, Makarius and Girard. Freudians agree that "Religion is the universal obsessional neurosis of humanity", as their founding-father put it. In *Totem and Taboo* he brought in the idea of the Oedipus Complex to explain the emotional intensity, the sense of guilt and the believers' sense of moral obligation to obey the alleged behests of the deity: it was all the result of the "primal horde's" crime of having slain (and probably eaten) their father, after having seen him as a rival for their mother's love. What masquerades as "religion" is nothing more than the sense of guilt and consequent obligation felt, to their slain father.

Objections: These focus on the simplistic and generalised conclusions that Freud "came" to, drawing a bit too uncritically from the questionable assertions of early evolutionists, like Darwin and Robertson-Smith. Even contemporary Freudians recognise that his Oedipus Complex theory was too hastily extrapolated by him to other cultural contexts. Finally, there has been a lot of rash over-generalisations by Freud from the behaviour of his neurotic and psychotic patients!

Conclusion: Religion is a curious mixture or positive and negative elements of healthy and unhealthy factors. Though wish-fulfillment, escapism and other regrettable ingredients are admittedly found there, we cannot dismiss all religion as "only that and nothing more".' As Bergson has pointed out, there are many psychologically sound believers. Still, religiously inclined people can make good use of Freud's insights and findings to purify their understanding of God and religion. So, the final verdict, after having reacted to the psychological attempts to disprove God's existence can only be "not proven"!

c. The Scientific Objection

History: This objection, for quite some time, had been gathering momentum with the tremendous advance and development of science in recent times. It was inevitable that this should have some impact on religion. However, with the advent of postmodernism and the realisation that scientific truths are not so smugly absolute, certain and universal as was once believed, the whole force of this argument has been blunted!

Formulation: Religion, so the argument goes, is nothing but a cloak for human ignorance. Thus, primitives, who had no knowledge of medicine for the physical sciences, felt constrained to postulate gods and spirits to explain many phenomena the sciences can account for. With the coming of the Renaissance in the fifteenth century and the information explosion in many spheres, especially astronomy, zoology, chemistry and physics it seemed that many issues – which churchmen had long thought was their exclusive sphere of control suddenly – were explained (if not explained away!) by people qualified in other disciplines! There were clashes between scientists and Judaeo-Christian leaders (heliocentrism, evolution, etc.) but it was invariably science that was proved right. All this has led many to wonder whether region is but a "harmless private phantasy" devoid of any real truth in any meaningful sense of the term. The argument seems to be compounded with the development of artificial intelligence (apparently de-throning the unique claim of humans to some kind of spiritual supremacy over the rest of "creation"), not to mention "cloning" (yes, religion is battling that, too...!).

Objection: It is true that religion has had to back down in many science vs religion controversies and has learnt to recognise that the Bible (and other revealed scriptures), if they do contain God's revelation, have clothed it in the very imperfect stages of scientific development that they had reached at the time. Of course, there are some "blind fundamentalists" who persist in asserting that everything in the Scriptures is literally true and must be believed so. They are an embarrassment to forward-looking believers and often indulge in fanatic, if not downright terrorist antics which bring discredit on religion in general and their religion in particular.

However, if one is convinced that belief in God is tied to the cultural presuppositions of a non-scientific age, then once these have been shown to be invalid, one's belief in God would collapse. But what if – as the latest developments in theology and scriptural study seem to bear out – what if God created an evolutionary world in which humans were allotted sufficient autonomy to relate freely to the divine, gradually and by painstaking research, slowly begin to make sense of their world and the cosmos – and in the light of this latter development, begin to grow in their understanding of God and God's word?

Scientific progress would be seen as part of the responsibility granted to humans and, against which background they must learn to grow into all-round mature adults, which includes the religious sphere.

Conclusion: Whether one sees scientific progress as a threat or contradiction to religious faith depends on how one's views both science and religion as well as how one's views their interrelationship. Thus, Scientific progress presents no real contradiction to religious faith.

d. The Fact of Evil and Wickedness

History: Perhaps the biggest stumbling block to belief in God, since time immemorial, has been the horrendous fact of the suffering of the innocent for no fault of their own. How can there be and all-good and all-powerful God – as all the theistic religions, at least claim there is – when the world is in such a mess? Apart from the fact of man-made ills (rape, murder and son on, the result of human free choice), which we could call "wickedness"!, there are also other awful events that bring a swathe of suffering and devastations in their wake – earthquakes, tidal waves, cyclones and epidemics – for which assuredly no human agency can be brought to book; we could reserve the name "evil" for such.

Formulation: Perhaps the most direct and poignant expression of this objection is found in the words of the third Century Roman thinker, Lucius Caecilius Firmianus Lactantius (c. 250-c. 325), who phrased it thus;

> God either wishes to take away evils, and is unable; or He is able and unwilling; or He is neither willing nor able, or He is both willing and able. If He is willing and is unable, He is feeble, which is not in accordance with the character of God; if He is able and unwilling, He is envious, which is equally at variance with God; if He is neither willing nor able, He is both envious and feeble, and therefore is not God; if He is both willing and, able, which alone is suitable to God, from what source, then, are evils? Or why does He not remove them?

Nearer to our time, David Hume, in *his Dialogues Concerning Natural Reason*[16] took up the objection in greater detail. More to his merit is the part of his treatise where he (in my opinion, quite successfully) showed that the principle of causality, upon which most proofs for God's existence depend, needs to be demonstrated and is not a "self-evident truth".

16 Hume, David. *Dialogues Concerning Natural Religion.* Dover Publications, 2013.

Objections: The "mystery of evil and wickedness" ranks as no mean difficulty in the path to "belief in God and theistic religions are very much aware of this, believing, as they do, in an infinitely loving and absolutely powerful God. Various attempts have been made by them to come to grips with the issue. Here, I will briefly advert to a few of them, taking up the challenge in more detail in a separate chapter devoted exclusively to this topic.

Dualistic Responses: This solution consists in seeing two rival ultimate powers in conflict, in effect, a "good god" and a "bad god": all evil is the work of the evil god (and his henchmen); all good is initiated by the good god and his angels and human followers. However, this "solution" but appears to solve on problem by creating another. It is evident that neither of the two protagonists is the "ultimate being": each is somehow limited by the other's presence and activity. Hence, neither of them can explain how they came to be! In ancient times, the Manichees (condemned as a heresy by early Christianity) taught such a view. In our own days, the Parsee religion, still alive in India today, whose prophet Zarathustra is said to have lived in the second millennium BC would seem to be a remnant of that faith, but in a much more advanced and developed stage.

Contemporary Hinduism: It has been well remarked that Indian religions take a "therapeutic rather than a metaphysical" approach to the scandal of suffering. In other words, their main concern is not what causes it or "Whence came the poisoned arrow?" but how to remedy and end suffering, "How to pull out the arrow?" Thus Hinduism and its derivatives, Buddhism and Jainism, teach asceticism, the control (if not the total extinction) of all desires and living in a state of unruffled peace and calm (shanti!). Indeed, the main object of yoga is not how to place one's limbs in all kinds of contorted positions, but to acquire total mastery of oneself, over one's body, passions, thoughts and desires. However, there is also an explanation for suffering, especially relevant in explaining the suffering of the innocent (babies born deformed, the treatment of untouchables and so on): in effect, the traditional solution is to say that these people are not really innocent. They are expiating, paying the punishment for, sins or faults committed in their previous life (this is the belief in reincarnation, once pretty widespread all over the face of the earth and still upheld by many Hindus, Buddhists and Jains, today). Reincarnation is a faith, let this be emphasised. It can neither be conclusively proved nor disproved. If one were to reject it, it would be more because of its implications, than any data against it. For example, reincarnation presupposes a body-soul dichotomy: in effect, my "body" is not really me – I can don or off it like I do my shirt or my shoes, while still retaining my identity. Besides, it implies a kind of resignation to one's lot. If I am deformed or denied my rights, I should not revolt against this: this is my karma. The only solution is to humbly submit to, and live out, my suffering and misery and in my next life I'll be reborn into a happier set-up. If this doctrine did provide moral motivation to many, it also bred a lot of passivity and resignation in the face of gross injustices that could have been overcome. Today, many committed Hindus, Buddhists and Jains are in search of a more, liberative interpretation of karma and rebirth. As for the occasional claims that this or that person has been able to recall his or her previous births, cases of fraud aside, the interesting and challenging study of Ian Stevenson, M. D., *Twenty Cases Suggestive of Reincarnation*[17] (cf. especially the case of Bridey Murphy) could, alternatively, be explained by ESP and, in any case, we know as yet very little about the powers of the human mind'!

Contemporary Christian Science: This view holds that evil is but an illusion of the human mind! I cannot but react strongly against this kind of answer and qualify it as the kind of feelingless response one can expect from people who've never known real prolonged pain and misery. Granted, some of our "pains" are psychological and there are psycho-somatic illnesses which can be cured by "mental power". But this is the kind of response one can expect from First World academics who've never had to know from inside, the agonies of one wasting away from cancer or AIDS, or experience racial or ethnic discrimination. Besides, it is not clear how this group can arrogate to itself the name "Christian" as the New Testament doesn't make any effort to underplay the harsh and ugly face of evil and presents Jesus as the victim of unjust cruelty, a veritable "suffering servant of God"!

The Boston "Personalist" School: This is the approach of thinkers like Edgar Sheffield Brightman (1884-1953) and some (not all) members of the "process theology" movement. They adopt the "easy way out" and deny God's infiniteness, postulating a finite deity battling with intractable matter. This kind of "God" is more humanly attractive – "Just like us, fighting by our aide!" – but, once again, we've solved one problem by creating another (bigger) one. For a "finite God" would be no God at all and would require an explanation as to how It came into existence (as finite, it could not be self-explanatory)!

Augustinian and Irenean Approaches: Augustine (354-430) and Ireneus (140-202) were both early Christian leaders who played an Influential role in the formation of Christian thought. Both were canonised not long after their death and both busied themselves with trying to respond to the objection against God's existence from the point of view of the evil in the world. Augustine's view, which is better known, was elaborated against a static world-view (the notion that God created a non-evolutionary world of finished products) and Irenaeus' vision, which is less known, is far more "mode", because it has a

17 Stevenson, Ian. *Twenty Cases Suggestive of Reincarnation*. Charlottesville u.a.: Univ. of Virginia Press, 2009.

more dynamic, evolutionary understanding of the world and worked out his "theodicy" (defence of God) from that perspective. Since I will be discussing their responses in a more detailed manner in a later chapter, I won't go into the issue now. Suffice would it be to point out that this objection is based on some questionable presuppositions. First, it assumes that the human person, as the rest of the reality that surrounds us, is viewed as having come forth from the hand of God as finished products. Secondly, the world is expected to be a place of maximum pleasure and minimum pain (a kind of kennel for God's pet, the human person). But if the world – and the human person –are viewed as Irenaeus does, as a place of person-making, fraught with hardship, inconvenience and danger, the only environment in which persons can grow into full maturity, then much of the objection crumbles. Besides, a whole lot of absurd and undesirable conclusions would follow from the "questionable presuppositons" I have outlined above. There would be no real need for work as no harmful consequences would follow. No science and technology would be possible as the laws of nature wouldn't always work in a uniform way (they would be suspended everytime they would work to human detriment) and there would be little or no scope for sacrifice, courage and higher morality, as everything would be made to work out well, by a divine agency.

D: General Conclusion

From the above it should be clear that we can neither definitively prove nor disprove God's existence. In effect, just as accepting God's existence (religious conviction) is basically a "faith decision", based on reasonable risk, atheism, too, is a matter of faith for it would equally be based on a reasonable risk!

"Homo sapiens, the only creature endowed with reason, is also the only creature to pin its existence on things unreasonable." –Henri Bergson

"The only hope I can see for the future depends on a wiser and braver use of the reason, not a panic flight from it." –F. L. Lucas

"The man who listens to Reason is lost: Reason enslaves all whose minds are not strong enough to master her." -George Bernard Shaw

"Men can be attracted, but not forced to the faith. You may drive people to baptism, you won't move them one step further to religion." –Alcuin

"If the work of God would be comprehended by reason, it would no longer be wonderful, and faith would have no merit if reason provided proof." Pope –Gregory, the Great

"Faith and Prayers are no substitute for Knowledge and Courage." –Joseph Lewis

Appendix to Chapter 3

FURTHER RELATED CLARIFICATIONS

a. On the Principle of Causality

The empiricist, David Hume, drew our attention to the fact that the "principle of causality" was used by two very different types of people for two very different purposes. There was first what he called the *empirical principle of causality*: this was used by scientists in their laboratories in order to discover and formulate scientific laws (e.g. Newton's Laws of Motion, Boyle's Law) or is presupposed when they take for granted how substances will behave within a particular set of circumstances, after having observed how they have reacted in the past (e.g. based on past observation, one can conclude that whenever an electric current is passed through a mixture of hydrogen and oxygen, water will be produced). He called this the "empirical" principle of causality because both terms of the principle, the antecedent, i.e., that which goes before (an electric current passing through a mixture of hydrogen and oxygen in the example above) and the consequent, i.e., that which comes after (water, in the same example) are both observable, which is what is meant by "empirical". Hume went on to say that there was no real reason to link the antecedent and consequent, other than psychological association (I've observed the two "going together in the past", so I assume that they will continue to do so in the future). This, admittedly, put science on a very shaky foundation and the scientist in Kant was quite appalled at the idea. He sought to provide a stronger link to the terms in empirical causality, but with little success. The details of how he did this are quite beyond the scope of this research work.

Then there was the *transcendental principle of causality* used by philosophers and theologians to "prove" the existence of God. They start with some observable phenomena in the world[18] and proceed thereby to argue to the existence of God (which is not observable or empirical but transcends or "goes beyond" our sense experience). Hume held that this was a quite illegitimate procedure and showed, quite conclusively, that its validity has to be established: it simply couldn't be taken for granted. Once again, the intricacies of Hume's reasoning are beyond our present scope.

It was left to Joseph Maréchal (1878-1944), a brilliant but unknown Jesuit priest and professor of philosophy at Louvain, Belgium, almost two hundred years later, to provide an insightful demonstration of the validity of transcendental causality, based on an analysis of our "intellectual dynamism", taking over where Kant had left off. The first thing Maréchal did was to work towards a more accurate, less careless formulation of the principle.

Careless Formulation No.1: This runs something like, "Whatever exists must have a cause." This provokes, inevitably, the following objection, "Well, if by your own admission, everything has to have a cause, why do you make a gratuitous, prejudiced exception for God? And if you're prepared to let him off the hook, why not let of other things as well?" This would result in embarrassed and mumbled apologies to the effect that this wasn't what was really meant.

Careless Formulation No. 2: In this version, one says, "Every effect requires a cause." This sounds a bit better. It even tells us why we need a cause for the world and not for God. God, unlike the world, is not an effect and so there is no reason why we should seek out a cause for God. But is this such an improvement after all? For, how can we know whether something is an effect or not, except by seeing it being made, observing its dependence on something else. And there's no way we can see the world depending on God!

Careless Formulation No 3: This is the one used by most philosophers, including Kant himself. It states that, "Whatever begins to be requires a cause." This is the most accurate formulation so far. But the first problem is that, in order to recognise that a particular being required a cause we would have to see its "beginning to be". Now that sort of thing can quite easily be done as regards babies, bushes and baskets, but not for the world as a whole. Besides, there is a deeper, metaphysical difficulty: as the formulation has it, only things which begin to be would require a cause. However, it can be shown there is no contradiction in the notion of an "eternal creation", that is, creation which has no beginning in time – and yet is created by God! Thus, even an eternal, beginningless creation would require a cause. Hence, it is not mere "beginning to be" but something subtler that is the criterion for causality!

An Accurate Formulation: This was proposed by Maréchal in the fifth volume of his *Le point depart de la metaphysique* (Brussels, 1949). It avoids the pitfalls of the other formulae and doesn't base itself on some other alleged

18 E. g. change, contingency, order, etc., as we saw in Aquinas' Five Ways.

principle of truth, either proved elsewhere or simply taken for granted. A simpler form than the one used by Maréchal would be, "A limited being as such, (i.e., by virtue of its very limitedness) depends totally on the unlimited being." Perhaps a word of explanation is required to clary what is meant by "total dependence". Let us take the traditional example of the carpenter (cause) and his table (effect). Now the table depends on its cause only for its "becoming", or "coming-into-being" as a table. It doesn't depend on him for its "staying-in-being": after he's made it, he can forget about it, go on his way and even forget about it – none of this will have any effect on the table! Nor does the raw material out of which the table as was made (wood, nails/ screws) depend on him; indeed, if they were not there, he wouldn't be able to make the table in the first place. Dependence , as being (or total dependence) embraces all these: coming-into-being, staying- in-being, the existence of the raw materials and so on.

What Maréchal does is to show, through an analysis of our "intellectual dynamism", evidenced through an in-depth study of "direct judgment" (i.e. the immediate affirmation or denial that something exists) that the unlimited being's existence is implicitly affirmed also. Furthermore, the dependence of the limited beings we know in this world on the unlimited being that transcends this world is equally asserted as a necessary precondition for the very act of doing this. A full exposition of Maréchal 's demonstration, interesting as it may be, is difficult to follow and presupposes at least an elementary knowledge of the basics of metaphysics.

b. Immanence and Transcendence

In traditional terminology, immanence refers to the inner presence, or "in-dwelling" of God within humans and, indeed, all things. In the Christian vision it is said that every human person is, thus, "a temple of the Holy Spirit". In the Hindu perspective, the Absolute is described as living in the depths of the cave of one's heart; ultimately it is even identified with one's deepest depths – *tat tvam asi*. Transcendence, on the other hand, reminds us that God is not simply "contained in" the universe, but overflows it, as it were. We can never fully attain God: God is beyond the farthest reaches of the distantest point in the universe. It has been observed that, in the Western tradition, the stress has been more on the quest for the transcendent deity, whereas in the Oriental tradition it is the immanent Godhead that is sought, by going deep into oneself. But this "inside-outside" vocabulary about God needs to be refined, somewhat.

Only material things can be located in specific places, inside, outside, in the middle and so on. Now, the immanence and transcendence issue is a far more subtler one than trying to "locate" God with reference to ourselves (and God is not a material thing!). Immanence refers to the inseparable bond that there is between God and all that exists: in Augustine's telling phrase,

"God is nearer to us than we are to ourselves." And having said this we must immediately bring in an important corrective: however close, intimate and inseparable be this bond between God and creation, the two cannot be identified. Were we to do so, all kinds of ridiculous conclusions would follow! Theism conceives of God as personally involved in the world, intimately and inseparably (immanence), yet it equally maintains that God remains distinct from all else that is (transcendence). Were one to accept immanence without transcendence, then one would have a pantheistic understanding of God (God and the rest of reality are basically one single being); on the other hand, were one to uphold only the transcendence of God, one would end up in deism (God is not involved with the world at all: there is no such thing as divine providence or conservation: in effect, God simply made us and, then abandoned us to look after ourselves).

c. God as Personal?

Classical Indian thought rejects the idea of a personal God – or so it has been said. This is a misconception, based on a wrong translation of *nirguna* and *saguna* as impersonal and personal. We are told, for example, that less enlightened people have need of a "*saguna* Brahman", while the more enlightened can appreciate the *nirguna* Brahman (wrongly translated as "impersonal Absolute" and "personal Absolute", respectively). But *nirguna* literally means "without attributes" and *sa-guna*, "with attributes". A God who is thought of as "having attributes or qualities" like we do – for we say that we have truth, goodness, beauty and so on – is a crassly anthropocentric one, narrowly conceived along human lines. To imply that God "has" qualities would be to make distinctions in God and mar God's unity. Rather, we say God is truth, goodness, beauty and so on. So, what the Indian sages were saying (and quite rightly!) is that we should avoid all unnecessary and exaggerated anthropomorphisms. Of course, inasmuch as we are humans, we cannot but think of God in some more or less anthropomorphic way (that is the limitation – and the glory – of our human condition). But we should ever be aware that we are using images, not meant to be taken literally and we should avoid crass anthropomorphisms which could mislead. Thinking of God as "a person", like we are, leads us to imagine that God's personhood is just like ours: God is peevish, jealous, possessive, moody, just like us and needs to be bribed, kow-towed to and so on – and lots of people behave just like this with regard to God. For these reasons, classical Indian thought has been wary of referring to God in personal terms.

But maybe we should pause for a moment to ask ourselves basically what we mean by a person. For example, all of us would instinctively hesitate to call a chair or a plant, or even a dog a person; we would have no hesitation in saying that any human being, regardless of sex, age, ethnic group, colour, creed and so on is a person. What does this reveal about what it means to be a person? Apparently, the fact that one is conscious at a deeper level and can freely enter into relationships of love and friendship. Well, even in the Hindu tradition, the Brahman (Absolute) is recognised as being *sat-cit-ananda* (being-consciousness-bliss). When we call God personal, what we mean is that God is no mere force, however powerful and efficacious God and forces may be for forces (e.g. gravity, electricity, atomic energy) are quite unaware of what they do. We mean that God is at least as (though, in reality, he is much more than!) aware as we are, as free as we are, as able as we are to enter into relationships. We do not mean that God is capable of love and of consciousness at the same imperfect level as we are. That is why it would be less misleading and more accurate to refer to God as personal, rather than "a person!"

d. A Few More Clarifications

We have already had occasion to introduce some oftenly used terms in the religious debate: theism, pantheism, deism, atheism and agnosticism. Let us round up this appendix with tying up all the loose ends in this regard.

Now, atheism (literally no-Godism) is the belief that there is no God. On the other hand, there is agnosticism (not-knowism), which holds that we do not have enough knowledge one way or the other to either affirm or deny God's existence. Scepticism (doubt-ism), in general, is the view that we humans are not able to attain any truths at all (this view is actually self-contradictory); in the religious sphere, a sceptic doubts God's existence and differs from an agnostic mainly in a matter of emphasis. Though "theism" is generally taken to be the belief that there is a God (as opposed to atheism), we have seen that there is good reason to give the name only to those who believe that God is both immanent and transcendent. If one believes in a God who is only immanent, that is pantheism (all-Godism): if one says God is only transcendent, that is deism. There is a more subtle position known as panentheism (all-in-Godism), which means that all things are in God and it is quite compatible with the theistic immanent and transcendent God. Then there is monotheism (one-Godism), which holds there is but one God, whereas polytheism (many-Godism) holds that there are many gods. Finally, there is also henotheism (single-Godism), which is a subtle variant of monotheism and 'polytheism. This is the belief that there are many gods, but restricts one's allegiance to the God of one's own tribe or clan. We tend to write off this last as belonging to the trash can of history but we have many examples of henotheism in today's world: jingoistic devotion to one's nation, the rush to amass power, wealth and prestige – all at the expense of other people and their convictions.

1. AQUINAS' FIVE WAYS

From St Thomas Aquinas, *Summa Theolgiae*. Ia, Q.2, art. 3, "Is there a God?"[19]

There are five ways in which one can prove that there is a God.

The first and most obvious way is based on change. Some things in the world are certainly in process of change: this we plainly see. Now anything in process of change is being changed by something else. This is so because it is characteristic of things in process of change that they do not yet have the perfection towards which they move, though able to have it; whereas it is characteristic of something causing change to have that perfection already. For to cause change is to bring into being what was previously only able to be, and this can only be done by something that already is: thus fire, which is actually" hot; causes wood, which is able to be hot, to become actually hot, and in this way causes change in the wood. Now the same thing cannot at the same time be both actually x and potentially x, thought it can be actually x and potentially y: the actually hot cannot at the same time be potentially hot, though it can be potentially cold. Consequently, a thing in process of change cannot itself cause that same change; it cannot change itself. Of necessity therefore anything in process of change is being changed by something else. Moreover, this something else, if in process of change, is being changed by yet another thing; and this last by another. Now we must stop somewhere, otherwise there will be no first cause of the change, and, as a result, no subsequent causes. For it is only when acted upon by the first cause that the intermediate causes will produce the change: if the hand does not move the stick, the stick will not move anything else. Hence, one is bound to arrive at some first cause of change not itself changed by anything, and this is what everybody understands by God.

The second way is based on the nature of causation. In the observable world causes are found to be ordered in series; we never observe, nor ever could, something causing itself, for this would mean it precede, itself, and this is not possible. Such a series of causes must however stop somewhere; for in it an earlier member causes an intermediate and the intermediate a last (whether the intermediate be one or many). Now if you eliminate a cause you also eliminate its effects, so that you cannot have a last cause, nor an intermediate one, unless you have a first. Given therefore no stop in the series of causes, and hence no first cause, there would be no intermediate causes either, and no last effect, and this would be an open mistake. One is therefore forced to suppose some first cause, to which everyone gives the name 'God'.

The third way is based on what need not be and on what must be, and runs as follows. Some of the things we come across can be but need not be,

19 Vol. II of the English Translation published by the Dominican Fathers of the English Province, Timothy McDermott 0. P., London, Blackfriars, 1963).

for we find them, springing up and dying away, thus sometimes in being and sometimes not. Now, everything cannot be like this, for a thing that need not be, once was not; and if everything need not be, once upon a time there was nothing. But if that were true, there would be nothing even now, because something that does not exist can only be brought into being by something already existing. So that if nothing was in being nothing could be brought into being, and nothing would be in being now, which contradicts observation. Not everything therefore is the sort of thing that need not be; there has got to be something that must be. Now a thing that must be, may or may not owe this necessity to something else. But just as we must stop somewhere in a series of causes, so also in the series of things which must be and owe this to other things. One is forced therefore to suppose something which must be, and owes this to no other thing than itself; indeed it is itself the cause that other things must be, and this everyone calls God.

The fourth way is based on the gradation observed in things. Some things are found to be more good, more true, more noble, and so on, and other things less. But such comparative terms describe varying degrees of approximation to a superlative; for example, things are hotter and hotter the nearer they approach what is hottest. Something therefore is the truest and best and noblest of things, and hence the most fully in being; for Aristotle says that the truest things are the things most fully in being. Now, when many things possess some property in common, the one most fully possessing it causes it in the others: fire, to use Aristotle's example, the hottest of all things, causes all other things to be hot. There is something therefore which causes in all other things their being, their goodness, and whatever other perfection they have. And this we call God.

The fifth way is based on the guidedness of nature. An orderedness of actions to an end is observed in all bodies obeying natural laws, even when they lack awareness. For their behaviour hardly ever varies, and will practically always turn out well; which shows that they truly tend to a goal, and do not merely hit it by accident. Nothing however that lacks awareness tends to a goal, except under the direction of someone with awareness and with understanding; the arrow, for example, requires an archer. Everything in nature, is directed to its goal by someone with understanding, and this we call God.'

2. MARÉCHAL'S VINDICATION OF THE PRINCIPLE OF CAUSALITY

a. The Method

Maréchal employs what is technically known as a transcendental analysis – analysing a given human activity with a view to exposing its necessary conditions. If the activity chosen is one that cannot be denied, then neither can anything which is shown to be its necessary pre-condition be denied either. Now, the activity Maréchal chooses for transcendental analysis is the most characteristic and basic act of the intellect – the direct judgment – and the direct judgment is an existential fact that cannot be really denied. Then we seek to uncover its necessary pre-conditions – and among these we will discover is the principle of causality, in its transcendental application (and a few other surprising things as well!) Thus, in a nutshell, will be our procedure – in reality, nothing more than carrying on to its fullest limits the analysis that Kant developed. However, due to his rather static understanding of knowledge, he wasn't able to reach Maréchal 's conclusions.

1. "Direct Judgment is a metaphysical fact."

By direct judgment is meant the immediate affirmation or denial that something exists. For instance, "This is a table", or "This is not a horse", are direct judgments. But "God exists", or "There is no such things as a soul", are not direct judgments, for they are not *immediate* affirmations; rather, they are conclusions we draw from other things of which we have had immediate evidence. Now, no one can deny that direct judgment exists for, his very act of denying it is an immediate affirmation – in other words, he/she is contradicting himself/herself: what is being said is being contradicted by what is being done. Direct Direct judgment, then, is an undeniable fact: we cannot deny that it exists. In Scholastic terminology, direct judgment is absolutely certain, undeniable (hence "metaphysical") fact.

2. "Direct .judgment is a movement, a dynamic process."

A little reflection on our experience of knowing should make this clear. We *want* to know. We are not indifferent to knowing or not knowing. *Avidva* or ignorance is a state repugnant to us. We want to get rid of it. Though we know that is not always an easy thing to attain truth, to get to know, we don't let that discourage us. We are prepared to struggle, to strive, argue and research in our attempt to know. So, knowledge is not just something that "happens to us from outside", that drops into our indifferent laps. Almost every knowledge we come by is the result of a definite wish, a real conquest, a conscious effort on our part. Knowledge is a difficult hut determined advance from ignorance through various stages, to certainty. *My intellect, therefore, is dynamic.*

3. "The Affirmation, in direct judgment, experiences a limit." Every direct judgment is couched in the from, "This is X," or "This is not X. In other words, in every direct judgment, we affirm two things about something: *what* it is (its essence, its 'this-ness') and *that* it is (its existence). Furthermore, a little reflection should make it clear that 1 don't recognise these elements as merely being juxtaposed, side by side. Rather, I experience the "is" element as actually limited by the "thisness" of the thing affirmed. Let me explain. When X affirm the "thisness" of something (i.e. what it is, its essence), I am affirming of it a quality that implies an inherent limitation: to be this means not to be that. To be a cow means not to be a horse, a man, a cat, etc. (="non-cow"). There are millions of things excluded by this negation. Essence, then, is a limitation in itself. But, the "is" element (existence) simply means "to be"; the only thing is opposes itself "to, or cuts itself off from, is "not-to-be", that is, no –thing. Thus, whenever I make an existential judgment (i.e., a direct judgment) and say, "This is an X", what I am doing is expressing the fact that the un- limitedness of "to be" is, in this situation, being restricted to being the "to be" of Just this "X". In other words, the dynamic movement of my intellect, *experiences* a *limit*, a check to *the dynamic movement* and process which we have shown (no. 2) to constitute the very nature of the direct Judgment.

4. "This means *that my intellect, in every direct judgment, is tending ultimately "towards the affirmation of the existence of the unlimited being.""* What is important, here, is to be aware of just *where* and *how* I am experiencing this limit. It is not that I am feeling dissatisfied with being confronted, here now, with a limited *essence*, with finding just so much of a particular essence (qualitatively and quantitatively) and, therefore, am "reaching out" for a "bigger and better" helping of the same, as it were. No! What I am reacting to is the limitedness of *existence* that I am encountering. This means that I am "reaching out" to the *unlimited existence*! When a movement experiences a block or a limit to its onward drive, this means that it trying to go beyond that limit. What is limiting the dynamism of my movement of affirmation is the fact that I am being held back by the *limitedness* of existence which, as we have seen is "in itself unlimited" (no. 3). In other words, I am tending towards pure existence, absolute and unlimited existence, unrestrained by any essence.

5. "The unlimited existence, ultimate goal of the movement of the Intellectual dynamism of my direct judgment, really exists."

We cannot argue from the mere fact that we are tending towards, or reaching out to, something that this thing actually Exists. Not every wish, want, or longing of ours, no matter how ardently we desire it with our whole being, entails an actually existing, or realisable, thing (or goal) to which we are tending. People have been known to strive for illusory, impossible ends. Wars have been fought, fortunes lost and lives gambled ... in vain to get hold of treasures (like the Philosophers' Stone, or the Garden of Paradise) that have never existed. Even Kant would grant that my intellect is made in such a way that it acts *as if* the unlimited being really existed. But, says he, this "unlimited existence" is merely an "ideal of reason": we cannot argue to its real existence from this mere tendency or movement. Hence, we need to show ' that this unlimited existence/being *really* exists. We may establish this along three distinct paths:

a) Starting from the reality of the observable world (this is more Maréchal's way). Either we accept that the world around is real, or we hold back from doing this (the Scholastic vs the Kantian position, respectively). If we follow the first approach (because, for instance, we find no valid reason enough to doubt our natural, spontaneous tendency to "take it" for real or because we find the objective reality of the world is the only reasonable and sufficient explanation for the "intentional" nature" of our affirmations, then there is no problem. For the unlimited being has emerged as the ultimate end of my intellectual activity and the limited beings of my daily experience are thereby manifest as mere proximate ends, stepping stones on my way to the unlimited being. Now, if the proximate, intermediary ends of my intellectual dynamism ("the things of this world") are real, as we have just established, all the more reason why the ultimate end should be real, for the intermediary ends have been shown to be partial realisations of the ultimate end. On the other hand, if we are dealing with Kantian agnostic (or others who also doubt the reality of the external world – the Buddhists, for example), then – as Maréchal argues – we could reason as follows. These people accept the immanent object as real (which is the proximate end of my intellectual activity), why do they refuse to go so far as to admit the real status of the exterior world or deny that our knowing can reach them as they are "in themselves"? *For,* if one is prepared to accept, categorically enough, that the immanent object is real, shouldn't one – logically and honestly – accept the reality of the unlimited being, since it has been shown to be one of the constitutive conditions of the same immanent object?

b) Starting *from the fact* that the unlimited being is not consciously sought: Some of our strivings or desires, as we have admitted, "are" conscious ones: we know what we are seeking after and deliberately try to attain them. I very consciously save up money to buy my dream house or study hard to secure a first class in my exams. It does happen that some of the goals that we consciously set for ourselves are unattainable or illusory goals, as when a tone deaf deaf person, with a voice like a frog, in spite of all advice, spends time, energy and money trying to become a pop singer! Then there are all those "quests" for the Philosopher's Stone, Paradise, El Dorado and the like. Some of our conscious (or "elicit") desires are naught but a wild goose chase, a pursuit of a wil-of-the-wisp, a search for idle phantoms that exist only in the deranged minds of us who seek them and nowhere in reality. But – and here is the rub! – all these illusory, false and mentally fabricated ends *always* belong to the area of our *elicit* or *conscious* desires! The deluded persons in question are fully aware that they are seeking Philosophers. Stones or whatever and they very consciously sacrifice all and strive with their might and main to attain those ends. But my striving after the unlimited being in all my intellectual activity is *not* a conscious or elicit desire! In fact, I am so unaware of it that a prolonged, interior analysis and critical reflection of what happens in the act of direct judgment is required to make me become explicitly conscious of it. The fact that I am not explicitly aware of it is a sign that I could not have concocted this end for myself! If its existence is not something I have invented for myself, that that is assuredly a sign that, since it exercises an attraction on me, it must exist independently of me!

c) Starting from the fact that the unlimited being is EXISTENTIALLY possible: I have deliberately high-lighted *existentially* inorder to distinguish this from St Anselm, tricked out in modern dress. Nothing be further from the truth. Our analysis has deduced the possibility of the unlimited being not from a mere analysis of the *concept* which is what Anselm did), but from "an undeniable *fact*, the activity of my direct judgment. Now, it is quite illegitimate to try and find "existence" as one of the "perfections" hidden in the *concept* of "most perfect being. For concepts belong to the order of essences, whereas existence belongs to a totally different order. One cannot have a concept of existence any more than one can hear a colour! Thus, analyse as we might, the concept of a "most perfect being" will never yield the quality of "perfection" of "to be" included there among the perfections of the essential order. But, in our analysis, we began with a real undeniable *activity* (direct judgment) and activity, like existence, belongs to the order of existence. This led us to the recognition of the *existential* possibility (as opposed to the mere *conceptual* possibility) of the unlimited being. Now, an unlimited being, if it is *existentially* possible, must exist. It cannot exist as a past or future possibility, but only as an actually existing existential possibility, for as pure unlimited existence, it has nothing else to limit its being!

6. "Therefore limited beings depend totally on the unlimited being." We have shown that the activity of direct judgment reveals that the things of our everyday experience are affirmed as partial realisations of the unlimited being, inasmuch as they are proximate ends, intermediary stepping stones on the path of our journey to the ultimate end. This means that they don't just happen be limited beings, while the unlimited is unlimited. Inasmuch as these beings, as limited, are partial realisations of the unlimited, and are discovered to be so in the analysis of direct judgment, this means that there is a real link of dependence of the former on the latter. They depend, as being (that is, totally), on the unlimited. Which is the same as the transcendental principle of causality!

b. Conclusion

It should be evident by now that, though we have validly established the principle of transcendental causality, there is no need to go all the way back to Aquinas' Five Ways to apply the now vindicated principle in order to get on with the job of "proving" God's existence. No need because God's existence is one of the things we have also discovered along with this principle! Thus, if the way of Maréchal has been a difficult and long journey, it has also been a an extremely fruitful one: it has not only vindicated a metaphysical principle of inestimable worth (and whose relevance extends to many very practical and down to earth areas as well); it has also led us to God as the ultimate goal of all our intellectual (and therefore human) activity. Finally, it also enables us – among other things – to recognise the created nature of "the things of this world"! A veritable "circuminsession of metaphysical verities", indeed!

3. THE "TWO WAYS" OF HERMENEUTICAL PHENOMENOLOGY

a. Introductory Notions

I do think that Hume, quite conclusively, has shown us that the principle of causality, in its "transcendental formulation", as he put it, cannot simply be taken for granted. In Aquinas' time, it was looked upon as a "self- evident truth" (*propositio per se nota*) and Hume pointed out how wrong this was. Furthermore, I do believe that Maréchal, quite successfully, took up the challenge of Hume and validated the principle. In the process, as we have seen, he also vindicated God's existence. However, I am also quite convinced that this approach, which appeals purely to the human intellect, would not be very relevant today. We would rather have a way of establishing God's existence which appeals to the whole human person and builds on the totality of human experience (something like the "greater probability" argument above). I would also like to humbly propose my own "two ways" based on the approach of hermeneutical phenomenology which, I think, are also more relevant to our modern personalist (and not to rationalist) frame of mind)

b. The Way of Our Quest for Meaning

Let me, at the outset, clarify that I am not presenting a somewhat modified version of Newman's argument for God's existence, starting from our moral consciousness. Just as he tried to show that moral consciousness must ultimately be grounded in God, I am saying that our quest for meaning ultimately is rooted in a quest for God. But I am *not* saying that only a believer in God can find meaning in life! I maintain that if we were to deepen our quest for meaning sufficiently, we would find God – as someone who had been walking by our side all along – not as someone who awaited us at the end of a long journey. The difficulty is that most people find so much meaning already in whatever (or whoever) has been the guiding light of their quest, that they feel no need to intensify their search. Thus, they miss the chance of going sufficiently into the experience and discover God as a fellow-traveller in their life's journey.

I am quite convinced that all of us are looking for meaning in life. Indeed, one might – for a moment, after a crushing tragedy or betrayal – be tempted to believe – and actually believe, for a while – that life is a cruel joke, " a tale of sound and fury, told by an idiot, signifying nothing, "But, after some time, our natural human dynamism comes into full play and we resume the pilgrimage to meaning. Were one to become convinced that life really has – and ever will have – no meaning on principle, he/she would come near to suicide! The human person is infinitely resilient and the worst of experiences, betrayals and frustration can't hold him/her down for long: sooner or later, we bound back into action for meaning!

Karl Jaspers has spoken of philosophical faith as a precondition of a sound philosophy, one which is based on authentic openness to reality. I would prefer to qualify this attitude as one of philosophical *respect*, an attitude of humble listening to, of reverence for, reality and what reality has to say. This is a far cry from the proud mentality with which many of our contemporaries bring to all that encompasses them, making selective observations, twisting and distorting facts to make them square with their favourite prejudices and then seeking to exploit and "bleed dry" their environment. My contention is that anyone who listens sincerely to our World cannot but acknowledge powerful intimations of transcendence. Now one of such intimations is linked to our quest for meaning. It is up to us to follow this through. One is not phenomenologically obliged to "see God in all" – "that is, there is nothing in what we observe that is of such nature as to oblige us to see God "at work" in the events that involve us. But it *hermeneutically valid* to do so. That is, it wouldn't be "flying in the face of evidence to the contrary" to do so, nor would this involve an illegitimate "reading into the data". If we allow ourselves to be borne along, both by the momentum of our inner dynamism as well as the "pointing beyond themselves" of "the things of this world", we cannot but admit that a theistic interpretation of the world is not even permissible but even invitingly plausible!

Viktor Frankl spoke of "the last of human freedoms" which no one can take away from us (unlike freedom of speech, movement, etc.) – "the freedom to choose one's attitudes in any given set of circumstances" which, for me, is the same as one's basic "freedom to make meaning" out of one's situation. And Frankl never wearies of quoting Nietzsche's telling statement: "He who has found a *why* to live for, can cope with any *how*.

It is "in and through" such key human experiences as the quest for meaning that we can encounter and discover God. As John Shea sums it up "Certain key experiences reveal the source and destiny of human life. In this revealing, the human experience is-not done away with but 'dwelt in and gone through' to what is beyond and yet within." And, once again, I interject that the quest for meaning is one such key experience.

God must be discovered "in and through" our experiences, as one who is "beyond and yet within": this by a valid hermeneutics, not a rational proof.

Maréchal, as we have seen, provides us a kind of metaphysical assurance of the legitimacy of such an interpretation. Rahner following his mentor, spoke of the *Vorgriff* (literally fore- or pre-grip, self-consciously translated by Donceel as 'transcending anticipation'). We discover that, in the last analysis, the only reason why anything other than God can give us meaning is because it is partly what God is fully!

c. The Way of Our Experience of "Contingence"

This is that other major intimation of transcendence open to us. It is pointed to by sociologists like Alvin Toffler, when mention is made of "Future Shock."[20] Briefly, he details how the phenomenon of change has become so radical, so universal and so swift that we are confronted with the future before we have had time to adjust to the present!

And when we turn to philosophers, there is perhaps none, East or West, who has written so poignantly and so perceptively of the discovery of contingence as Jean-Paul Sartre. His arresting existential vocabulary lays bare the horror he experiences as he chances upon it.

In his autobiographical *Nausea*,[21] young Roquentin (= Sartre) tells of his terrible realisation that contingency leers at him through the roots of a chestnut tree in the famous Luxemburg Gardens in Paris. The obscene and brutal fact *of* the roots of the tree plainly and simply being there, without offering any explanation as to why is should be there at all, is what revolts and disgusts him. Then he comes to the slow and gradual horrific discovery that this is true not only of the roots of the chest-nut tree but of everything he encounter the bench he is seated on, the ground on which he stands. ... even himself: everything merely is; nothing can explain why it is, rather than is not! Everything is gratuitous, contingent: it could just as well not be. All is de *trop*, superfluous. In Roquentin-Sartre's own words:

> Contingence is everything. I mean that, by its very definition, existence is not necessary. To exist is simply *to be there*: existents appear, let themselves be encountered, but one can never *deduce* them ... Everything is gratuitous, this garden, this city and I myself ... That is nausea!

Sartrean nausea is much more than a physical repugnance from the contact with things. It is, rather, as Brian Master's puts it, "an affective repugnance progressing to a seizure of intellectual horror at the valueless, worthless character of existence." From this recognition of contingence – the basic metaphysical insufficiency of the things of this world (including one's own self) – a whole gamut of negative feelings are provoked in Sartre: fear, anguish, disgust, loathing, anger.

---

20 Toffler, A. *Future Shock*. New York: Bantam Books, 1996.

21 Sartre, J.-P. [Bronx, N.Y.] : Ishi Press International, 2018.

The realisation that we are free is, of course, some initial consolation. "I am free!" exults Orestes in the play *The Flies*.[22] "Freedom has burst upon me like a thunderbolt. ... Once freedom has exploded in the soul of man, the gods can do nothing against him!" But we soon realise that freedom brings along_ with it such an awesome and frightening responsibility that it can only plunge us back into the blackest depths of despair and loneliness. In fact, most people shy away from it and seek, through various dishonesties, alternative escapist ways to evade this responsibility.

But Sartre didn't seem to have realised that his pessimistic outlook was but one possible conclusion to draw from the experience of contingence. He argued, in effect, "The roots of the oak-tree/all observable things/ I myself exist gratuitously. Yet all of these do exist. Therefore, all is meaningless, absurd..." But there is another way of proceeding, of equal hermeneutical validity, for it is an alternative interpretation which takes all the facts into consideration, equally! It would run something Like this: "That roots of the oak-tree/all observable things/I myself exist gratuitously. Yet all of these do exist. Therefore, they must have been gratuitously loved into existence!" The existence of things cannot be accounted for out of some rational necessity; perhaps, then, gratuitous love could explain why they do exist at all I If we can find no rationally satisfying ground for the existence of things, might this not point towards an alternative meta-rational justification for their existence – love? Cosmic necessity, metaphysical demands – none of these can explain why things are. Whatever explanation one manages to come up with, it would have to partake of the gratuitous. Chance is one such explanation, hermeneutically valid (but repugnant and nauseous to Sartre). But does not gratuitous love equally fit the bill? Gratuitous love would account for the fact of contingence, as much as offensive gratuitous chance! I am. I exist. But there is no metaphysical reason why I should exist. Therefore, I have been loved into existence.

This is not the type of argumentation that traditional rational philosophy is built on; but it is "the way of proceeding" of hermeneutical phenomenology. It is as valid a hermeneutical conclusion from the facts as is Sartre's absurdity thesis. Sartre was right in saying that existential despair is *one* possibly valid interpretation of the undeniable experience of contingence; he was wrong in assuming that it was the only possible hermeneutical response to that datum.

Faced with two equally valid interpretations of the same data (both equally explain all the facts, without exaggerating or omitting any aspect of them), how do we decide which one to opt for? All we can do to suggest guidelines to answer a question like that is to point to two commonsensical practical helps; (i) look for some evidence (even if it is not absolutely cogent) in favour of the

22 Sartre, J.-P. (2014). *The Flies*. New York: Spark Publishing, 2014.

"reasonable risk" involved in your preferred stance, (ii) choose that preferred stance which resonates with your personal world view and value-system. Now, among other things (and quite a few of such, at that), Maréchal gives us a very reasonable basis in favour of this hermeneutical stance. For he has shown us that the things of our daily experience (including ourselves) are not sufficient unto themselves, ontologically, that is, as being. They cry out for Something, Someone (?) in which they can rest and have their continued being.

Nor, should it be noted, that I justifying every "leap into God" that would launch itself off from each and every experience of human insufficiency – physical, psychological, etc. The experience of physical-insufficiency should drive us to seek completeness in humans and in sub-human reality; awareness of psychological insufficiency should lead us to deeper companionship with other persons. It is only in the sphere of *metaphysical* insufficiency that we are justified in making a direct leap into God!

Is there any difference in this approach of mine and Aquinas' celebrated "third way" of proving God's existence? The comparison is understandable, but one really cannot reduce my "second way of hermeneutical phenomenology" to the "third way" of Aquinas. Aquinas' is a proof that stands or fall with the truth of the major or minor as well as the validity of the reasoning which holds them together. My way is not by means of rational proof but a manner of interpreting phenomena. And God is not found waiting at the end of the process (as in Aquinas', by virtue of causality); rather he is discovered as having been accompanying us all along, walking by our side. My way consists basically of showing that it is hermeneutically valid to suggest that reality is here at all as a result of love.

Of course, Sartre might dismiss all I have said as idle nonsense. On the other hand, I can retort that the ontology to which I subscribe is an interpretation of facts, at least as much valid as Sartre's! His interpretation, as well as mine, is a valid approach.

"Religion? Let us talk of it less and practise it more!" –Sadhu Vaswani

"Every man thinks God is on his side. The rich and powerful know that he is." –Jean Anouilh

"It were better to have no opinion of God at all, than such an opinion as is unworthy of him." –Francis Bacon

Chapter 4

SYMBOLS, MYTHS AND RITES

Introduction

Symbols, myths and rites seem to have a bad press in today's world. For many people they seem to be very part and parcel of the whole panopoly of religion in general and of cult in particular. The every mention of the words appears to conjure up unpleasant memories of obscurantism and superstition. And the Fact that all of these, in varying degrees, seem to be on the way out in the more "enlightened" societies, is often construed as a good sign ... and good riddance!

However, a closer and more critico-reflective approach might lead us to wholly different conclusions. We will discover that, perhaps, we can no more outlaw symbol, myth and rite from our lives than we can banish our own bodies! Indeed, to think that we can – or even try to do so – often contributes to our own mental malaise. Besides, as we shall see, it is not true that symbol, myth and rite belong exclusively to the realm of religion ... even though they are a potent means to help people move from belief that to belief in!

1. Symbols

a. Origins

Historically, the word symbol is derived from certain usages in ancient Greek society, which were finally incorporated into legal practice. A correspondence between broken pieces of a vase or tablet served to identify bona fide guests to a party. Later on, the practice was used to identify which members of Athenian society had a right to vote in the agora. Each of the above- mentioned fragments was called a symbol (Greek, *sym-ballo* = I throw something together with something else).

From the above we can say that a symbol was originally something tangible that referred to, or called to mind, something else which was, at least tangibly, absent. But this "definition" is a bit vague and would hardly serve to distinguish a symbol from a sign in general.

Towards a More Scientific Definition

To make a long story short, all symbols are signs but not all signs are symbols. What they both have in common is that they are tangible things that refer to something other than themselves, which are either abstract or not tangibly present. Where they differ is how they do this referring, or calling to mind.

The eminent French phenomenologist, Paul Ricoeur, defines symbol which gives us a precise glimpse of how this is done. A symbol, he says, has a double intentionality (for practical purposes, we can equate this word with "meaning"): one is primary and more direct, the other secondary and indirect. Most important: the second intentionality is conveyed through the first!

Let us clarify this somewhat abstruse explanation by means of a simple example. Take the dove. The primary and direct meaning of the word is, a bird, a common enough bird, well known in just about all countries and cultures. The secondary and indirect meaning of dove is peace. A dove symbolises peace and it does so because the dove shares in, or evokes, some quality of peace, namely gentleness and calm (this is how "the second intentionality is conveyed through the first"). Thus, if one contemplates a dove, moving about quietly and serenely on its business, gradually a feeling of peace and tranquillity would descend on one. A dove can symbolise peace because it shares in, or evokes, qualities of peace. That is why a hawk, or some rapacious bird of prey, cannot "symbolise" peace!

And this is the fundamental difference between a symbol and other signs. A mere sign is a pointer. One must not focus on it, but go beyond it, in order to arrive at what is signified. A sign is not the signified, to linger ones attention on it would miss the bus! We must look beyond the pointing finger to the star. However, for a symbol "to work", we must pay attention to it, contemplate it. As Ricoeur liked to say, a symbol provides food for thought (*donne à penser*). If a sign has a merely indicative function, the symbol has a revelatory function. The sign asks us to go beyond itself and come to what is signified? the symbol asks us to focus on itself and thereby it somehow "makes present" what it symbolises.

b. Symbols and Idols

Having distinguished the symbol from the mere sign, we must straightaway set it apart from the idol. For the idol, like a symbol also seem to be efficacious: it also claims to do something, to make present something absent or make tangible something intangible. Once again, the difference lies in how they do it! While the symbol evokes that which it symbolises, the idol claims to have encapsulated, entrapped within its slender confines that which it refers to. The symbol recognises that there is a "surplus" above and beyond what it has rendered present. It merely apprehends, or just manages to put us in touch with the symbolised – just reaching – it with our finger-tips, as it were. The idol, on the other hand, by encapsulating what it refers to, claims to have com-prehended or completely grasped – within the fist, as it were – what it refers to. There is no elusive "surplus" that escapes the idol's clutches. Indeed, most of our problems arise because we, or someone else, have let symbols imperceptibly and carelessly degenerate into idols. To quote, Ricoeur once more, "Idols must die so that symbols can live!"

c. How Do Symbols "Work"?

From the preceding it should be evident that symbols are efficacious: they act, they do something. And what they do is render present or tangible something which is absent and/or intangible. They do this by sharing in, or "participating in" some quality of that which they symbolise. I prefer to say, with some other thinkers, that they share a "common rhythm" with it. But I have a qualification to offer: one must perceive this common rhythm, else the symbol will not be able to work! There is a strong vein of subjectivity that undergirds the symbol's efficaciousness. For instance, for most of us, time is linear: it flows on and never returns. That is why for most of us a stream is the ideal symbol for time: both are characterised by the "common rhythm" of linear, non-reversible movement. In classical Indian thought, however, time is traditionally seen as cyclic, circular, as caught up in an endless, repetitive round. Thus, for the seers of the Rg-Veda. the stream (or river), i.e., a symbol of the journey of all beings to the Absolute and the wheel is the symbol of time. Again, for the English speaker, the owl is a symbol of wisdom; but for the average Indian, the owl (*ullu* in Hindi) symbolises stupidity. For some mysterious reason, an Englishman sees a "common rhythm" between the owl and wisdom, whereas the Indian sees it as sharing or "participating in" some quality of stupidity!

d. Why Do We Need Symbols?

When we are separated from someone we love dearly – either by distance or by the person's death – we invariably treasure a photograph of that person or a memento from him/her (a lock of hair, a letter...), anything tangible that would personally link us with the loved one in some tangible way. In moments of crisis or fear, we might even find ourselves clutching the object to our breast or even kissing it! That object is functioning "symbolically" for us: it helps us to tangibly sense the presence of someone who's tangibly absent.

Nor are we satisfied with "loving our country in the abstract". From time to time, we must take out a parade, march past, and salute the flag, wave it, carry it aloft and, on occasion even kiss it. And we would feel outraged were someone to spit on it or trample it under foot (just as we would, were someone to mete out the same treatment to our loved ones photograph)! Our national flag is much more than "a piece of cloth on a stick": it is a symbol of our country; its colours and devices, somehow, "participate" in the history and ideals of our land and, as we contemplate it, our hearts swell with love for it.

These two examples should suffice to explain why we need symbols. Symbols serve to make the intangible tangible, the absent present. And, precisely because we are embodied beings, we feel the need to relate holistically to whatever is important and precious to us. Hence, our bodies and senses must, in some way or the other, be allowed to enter into such relationships or we feel frustrated. We're no angels and a body-less love-affair, one that leaves so essential a dimension of ourselves out of the picture, is doomed to frustration. Hence, we need symbols. Someone who has no place for symbols in his/her life is someone who is not taking his/her body seriously ... and is well on the way to, at least, serious neurosis. Even religions like Judaism and Islam, which frown on images in worship allow for some symbolic representation of their faith: the Star of David and the Crescent, respectively. Symbols lend a certain tangibility and personal touch to an otherwise totally intangible divinity. The problem arises when we believe or act, as if the divinity were looked up in the symbol so as to become totally identified with it – and hence resists all attempts to change an outdated or irrelevant symbol which, in another age or in another place, cannot "deliver the goods". This is idolatry of symbols!

2. Myths

a. What Do We Mean by "Myth"?

If a symbol is an object, a myth is a symbolic story. Unfortunately, for most people, a "myth" is a synonym for untruth, a lie. Thus, people assert that, "The inevitable progress of mankind is a myth!", meaning that such an idea is false. That is why religious believers tend to take offence and become defensive if they are told that myths play an important part in their faith life. Indeed, some people would go so far as to say that myths might have been useful "once upon a time", when humans were "primitive", "unenlightened" and so unable to digest abstract philosophical truths. Hence, to facilitate their understanding and assimilation by such underdeveloped minds, they had to be couched in stories. That would render the abstruse doctrine more digestible to the uneducated natives' brains. Nowadays, however, they argue, we are more developed and can go in directly for the raw meat of complicated philosophico-theological dogma and need no airy-fairy stories of, say, Adam and Eve and a talking snake!

This patronising attitude stems from a rationalistic bias. It is assumed that the only proper way to view things is by means of the detached, objective way of the sciences, making use of concepts and reason. No, there is no denying that the scientifico-technological approach to reality is a very valid and – useful one and has done a lot to improve our lifestyles and our standard of living. But there comes a time when we need to pay attention to the subjective side of knowing, stressing how things come across to me, the knower, through affectivity. We need to occasionally complement our distanced, objective way of understanding things through concepts with a more involved, subjective manner, using the affectivity.

b. What Is the Value of a Myth?

Myths are symbolic stories which throw light upon who we are, where we are heading and how we "fit in" to the scheme of things. However "modern" we may be and however much our generation may have "come of age" – particularly if it is a highly technocratic society that we have grown up on – we need to cultivate and feel a "sense of belonging." And that is precisely what a functioning myth does.

A myth needs not be a true story, but it always contains more truth than a true story. I, for one, am one of those who do not hold that the Adam-and-Eve myth (revered by three of the world's great religions, including mine) is historically true. I do not believe that the Adam and the Eve of the story really existed or that the serpent spoke to them in their language. The whole story is "made up", but it contains some important truths and this is where, I think, a believer must seek to locate God's revelation. And it is presented in a story form, not because it would have been unintelligible to the allegedly then "primitive minds" to whom it was originally addressed, but because a story is the best way to communicate a sense of belonging – and that is what the myth is trying to do, by inviting us to identify with the *dramatis personae*! The purpose of the "Adamic myth" is not to give us precise scientific information as to how the world (or man, or woman) came into existence, but what man, woman and the rest of creation is and how they were supposed to relate to each other. It is not trying to tell us "how" sin began ("original sin") but explain to us what sin is and what it does to us and our relationships with each other and the world. A well-researched biography may be a "true story", but it is not relevant to me. It doesn't throw light on my life. If I accept the Adam and Eve myth, which is not basically a true story, I recognise that it is telling me some very relevant truths about myself, where I have come from and where I'm heading, how I should act in today's world: it contains more truths than a true story! People who reject the Adam and Eve tale because of objections like, "How can a snake talk?" have missed the point of it all. Aesop's fables and the parables of Jesus lose nothing of their contemporary relevance as to the timely "home truths" they challengingly tell us because they were not historically true and were invented by their narrator! Psychologists today are of the opinion that one of the many reasons why "modern man" feels alienated, "lost in the crowd," forlorn in the concrete jungle, is because he has no meaningful myths to give him a sense of belonging to his world.

Every nation has its myths. How else could a motley group, stemming from such diverse cultures and religions and speaking such different languages, like the citizens of India derive a feeling of national solidarity? So we Indians have our *Ramayana* and *Mahabharata*, just as the ancient Romans had their Aeneid, the Greeks of old their Odyssey and Iliad. The Germanic peoples have their own *Niebelungslied*, the French *La chanson de Roland* and the Portuguese *Los Lusitanics*.

The life of Karl Marx had mythic value for Marxists, the exploits of Chairman Mao is myth for a committed Chinese Communist, just as the life of Jesus functions as a myth for a believing Christian!

3. Rites

a. What is a Rite?

A rite is a symbolic action. Some people wish to define rite as a "myth in action," but that is the kind of rite you would find being enacted in temples, churches and when people are doing something specifically religious. But not all rites are religious. Some are secular. Sometimes it's not easy to draw a hard and fast line between the two. Taje, for instance a marriage rite or a funeral rite. Obviously, these have both a religious and a secular (human, social) overtone. It's often more a question of emphasis and occasionally a rite has one foot planted squarely in each camp.

b. What is the Value of Rite?

This is tantamount to asking, why do we need rites? Rites are actions which give us a sense of belonging in a given society, something very important for us social beings. Secular rites initiate us into a given human society or, at key moments in our life, reinforce that sense of belongingness. This latter is also important for, as we undertake new responsibilities in society, we feel somewhat overawed, if not downright scared! The rite assures us that we are not alone, that there is a community standing by our side at such moments, assuring us of support and solidarity! In a religious rite, through the mediation of a community to which we belong, we are led to an encounter with God, the Ultimate Reality, with what really matter for us.

c. Secular Rites

For convenience, let us break up secular rites into greeting rites and rites of passage. Greeting Rites as the name suggests, sore actions that express amity and welcome, either between two unknown persons or between old friends. Handshakes, an upraised right hand, the "*namaste*" and embraces – these are the most common examples! These gestures, decided upon by convention express, sometimes reinforce, friendship. At the minimal level, they at least manifest non-animosity!

Why do we need rites at all? For the simple reason that we need some exterior manner of making our innermost (and, therefore, secret) feelings tangible and manifest, giving them communitarian import! How else, indeed, would our friends come to know our deeper, truer selves and our states?

Furthermore, even when these feelings have been made known to others (as when a boy has declared his undying love to a girl), we still feel the urge to renew such ritual expressions from time to time. Firstly, such "renewals" affirm that the passage of time and the ups and downs of the relationship have not broken, or even harmed, the commitment? which does remain a sad possibility! Strictly speaking, then, these "repeated" gestures and not really repetitions, after all, they are affirmations that, whatever has come to pass since the time they were last expressed, the bond of love or friendship has not been affected – except, perhaps, to have become deeper and more mature. Thus, far from being a soulless repetition, they are a communication of an abiding commitment, a reaffirmed self-giving, an enduring relationship! This point is to be borne in mind when encountering the oft-repeated objection that religious rites are "merely repetitions"! Secondly, affectivity, like knowledge – indeed, even more so – cries out for expression! If unexpressed and unshared knowledge is frustrated knowledge, all the more is unexpressed and unshared affectivity.

Then there is that very large and complex category of rites, usually called rites of passage. This comprise all those *rites of passage* which celebrate key events in one's life, milestones whereby we make a transition or passage from one life to another, or assume newer and more demanding responsibilities. Among the more striking are birth, or initiation, rites and, finally, funeral rites. Those celebrate one's incorporation into a community and, after passing through the different phases in one's life-journey, one's last mysterious passage into the thereafter. In between, there are rites to mark one's growth (birthdays), one's passage from childhood to puberty and thence to adulthood, from the single to the married state as well as the assumption of important offices and responsibilities. All these are aimed at giving a person a sense of belonging, as also assuring him/her of further support from the community as he/she is progressively incorporated into society at deeper levels, taking up ever more exacting and, perhaps, frightening responsibilities, as time goes on.

d. The Modern Anti-Ritual Prejudice

Mary Douglas lamented what she felt was a "world-wide revolt against rites" and averred that "one of the gravest problems of our day is the lack of commitment to popular symbols." This has resulted in our breaking up into smaller and smaller private groups, closed in on themselves, each with its own private system of individualistic symbols, suspicious and wary of all other groups and rites. Counsellors, like Rollo May, have hazarded the opinion that the explicit rejection of symbols and rites have caused not a few mental disorders today.

But can we really "throw out" so successfully all symbols and rites from our life? As much as we drive them out of the front door, -they -tend to creep in from the back! Mircea Eliade reminds us of the number of apparently secular festivals and celebrations that preserve "a strong mythical structure:" "the rejoicings over a New Year" (millenium?), or the rites "following the birth, of a child the building of a house, or even the removal into a new flat." Don't all these smack of our yearnings for a new beginning, a complete regeneration? Can we not also recognise mythic and ritual roots (especially the "re-living of a myth in action") in most public spectacles, from theatre way past the viewing of one's favourite "soaps", down, to athletic contests and sports (from bull-fighting down to the Olympic Games and the World Cup)? In all of these, there is that sense of highly concentrated time, occasionally the weird feeling that we have "caught up with the future" or a "reliving the past as present", all of which characterise religious ritual and gave these experiences a kind of magico-mystical sensation. Even reading novels and going to the movies give us heroes and villains, to identity; or dissociate ourselves with. We share in their labours and triumphs, live out the eternal and universal motifs of their struggle and triumph, along with them in their eschatological moments, experiencing a kind of vicarious resurrection and salvation.

"Myth embodies the nearest approach to absolute truth that can be stated in words." –Coomarswamy

"Hitherto this function (of the symbol) has been but little analysed, worthy as it is of deeper study..." –Immanuel Kant

"The rite is not simply one type of action among others, it is the typical human action." –Louis Bouyer

Chapter 5

THE RELIGIOUS LEADER

a. Introductory Remarks

It is a sad fact (to put it mildly) that religious leaders down history, who are supposed to facilitate our encounter with God, have very often (not ways!) done just the opposite. More often than not, these men (the gender slanted term is deliberate) are male chauvinists, conservative to the worst degree, old and frightened ancients who are the exclusive custodians of religious institutions and the privileges they enjoy thereby. And call them what you will – priests, pastors, preachers, pujaris, imams, shamans, bonzes, rabbis, witch-doctors or what not – much of what is justly opposed or condemned in organised religion is the fault of certain unscrupulous and oppressive members of this motley crew, whose arrogant claims and despotic behaviour are the main cause of the distrust and distaste of many people for organised religion in general and its officials in particular!

b. Priestly vs the Prophetic Paradigm

Religious leaders, for practical purpose, may be sub-divided into two main types, the priestly and the prophetic. The former are characterised by their understanding that they have a cult to perform, the latter by the conviction that they have a word to speak. The distinction, like many distinctions, is not always very precise: it's often a question of emphasis and a matter of situating a particular religious official more at one end of the spectrum than the other. But precisely where the emphasis is perceived to lie makes a very big difference for all concerned.

The Priest, in the history of religions, is a cultic figure. His role is to ensure that the proper and prescribed way of worshipping the divinity is carried out at the required time(s). One becomes a priest, either by being a male born into some priestly caste (e.g. Brahmin) or tribe (e.g. Levi), or by undergoing a ceremony called ordination. The priest was originally seen as the great mediator between the all-holy God and us all-sinful human. He was, ideally speaking, the *pontifex maximus* – the great bridge-builder across that awesome abyss. The main function of the priest was "to take us (lesser mortals) to God and bring God to us." None but these specially set-apart "bridges" could dare fulfil this indispensable mediatory role. None but they were reputed to know how to do the job – what precise words to pronounce and when, which particular rubrics to follow in the process of prayer and worship. No mere "layman" could arrogate to himself this mandate: the priest was the only authorised intermediary to assure us of God's blessings, bring down curses on one's enemies and guarantee us divine forgiveness for our sins ... all at a generous fee, of course.

Furthermore, to ensure that there'd be minimum scope for blasphemous, ambitious and rebellious outsiders usurping his priestly prerogatives and tasks, the rules governing valid rituals became more and more elaborate – and meticulous exactitude was demanded in the entire process – failing which, the whole process would be rendered null and void, if not invalid: thus nigh months (years?) of practice would be required before one could "get it right!" In addition, the language in which the official prayers were couched had to be, more often than not, some recondite, "sacred" language, the study of which was sometimes restricted under pain of death to the clerical coterie. In the end, the priest emerged as more powerful than God: he alone knew how to oblige the divinity to his priestly will, by pressure of the right usage of word and gesture!

The Prophet (literally, a spokesperson) has not so much a rubric to execute as a message to proclaim. The prophet can be of any sex, social group or community. Whereas the priest's role was usually understood as to coax a whimsical divinity to do as he directed, the prophet's function was seen as just the opposite: interpreting God's word and, thence, calling the people to action and change of heart. Prophetic figures are discernible in all religions ... and outside of them, too. At least two of the most hearkened to prophets of our time – Karl Marx and Ernesto "Che" Guevera – were not even religious believers. But, if the great prophets have ever summoned people to action for justice and liberation, there have also been "false prophets", time-serving demagogues who would enlist their oratorical talents in favour of the status quo, or to acquire and consolidate dictatorial power. There have been prophets like Hitler who, cleverly "interpreting" the 'signs of the times', sent their people off on a mission of genocide and riot! Let us never underestimate the creative power of human beings. We have the uncanny ability to distort or reorient the noblest of ideals for the shoddiest of purposes!

c. Two Kinds of Identity

There are two common approaches to establishing one's identity, *identity by exclusion* and *identity by inclusion*. Normally when a person or a group experiences an "identity crisis", the problem is usually dealt with by making a list of exclusive functions which only that person or group have a right to perform, thus setting them off or "identifying" them from everyone else. It seems to me that this is a very immature way of defining oneself: in terms of jealously safeguarding some alleged privilege or power which devolves to one's exclusive self, setting one apart from everyone else.

The usual way in which the priest – for example the Catholic priest – has understood "identity" is as follows: He has considered himself as having received, through his "ordination", certain "powers" which he has the exclusive right to exercise and which no lay person can assume (e.g. only a Catholic priest can "forgive sins" and effect the transubstantiation at Mass). The list of such exclusive powers or functions was once quite lengthy. Nowadays! that list has shrunk quite a bit, as lay people have been granted a share in many activities and ministries once considered the sacrosanct right of then priest alone (Catholic laity can now become Eucharist ministers, lectors, married deacons and so on). No wonder the Catholic priest, accustomed to an "identity by exclusion" has experienced an identity crisis and there is a "decline of vocations!"

Perhaps the best way for me to explain what I mean by "identity by exclusion" is through the example of the soldier. All citizens of a country – both civilians as well as members of the armed forces – are expected to love their homeland and, to the best of their ability, defend it against the depredations of the aggressor. But that is a responsibility of such vital importance that it becomes necessary to set aside certain citizens (either as conscripts or as volunteers for the job) to devote their time and energy to undergo the rigorous training and discipline that would ensure the task be done most effectively. Thus, some of us, either as a result of our own inner choice, or as the outcome of canvassing, present ourselves as candidates for the Army, Navy or Air Force. Those who finally "make it" to the marching out parade, commissioning, or whatever, do not thereby receive any specially exclusive powers that are denied to "the man in civvy street". It's just that they have been more thoroughly prepared to fulfil a serious responsibility in a manner more effective, than the average, untrained person would be. What distinguished the trained soldier from the civilian is not that the former has certain powers and privileges which the latter has not, but that the member of the armed forces has been formed to be a far more capable defender of his country than the civilian – who also shares in that same responsibility. It is along these lines that we should seek to understand the identity of the religious leader.

The more the religious leaders tends to think of himself as a priestly or cultic official, the more he will tend to seek to boost his flagging identity by jealously guarding his alleged- preserve of exclusive powers and lording it over his "flock" which, to all the world, he treats as if it had the brains of sheep! The prophetic leader sees himself/herself as having no unique or special powers: he or she has been simply given a formation that would best help him/her to discern and interpret the word of God and present it to his/her people. But the people also share in this responsibility of hearkening to God's word and interpreting it amid the signs of the times, for God doesn't speak only through his specially trained prophets: all the people share in the prophetic vocation, all have to help make God's word come challengingly alive in their context. And why should the "prophet" be upset if "laypeople" shoulder part of the burden? The prophet, with all his/her training is not rendered thereby infallible and the lay-person with all his/ her insights and faith experience has the right to question the word of "the prophet" as the entire community struggles to discern what God is staying in the here and now.

d. Hierarchic vs Democratic Structures

Traditional religious leadership has been based on a hierarchic structure, i.e., one in which all power is deposited in a supreme authority figure, who has received it directly from God. If secular rulers have long abandoned the "Divine Right of Kings" theory, whereby any disobedience to the civic authority was construed as disobedience to God, hence blasphemous and meriting the worst forms of penal sanction, religious leaders, by and large, still cling to it, tenaciously. They, believe that they are part of a Sacred Order (which is what "hierarchy" means) with a strict protocol and pecking order to be observed in the process of command and authorisation. How much power and privilege is enjoyed by any member of the organisation depends strictly on (the whims and fancies of) the next higher-up in the chain of command. There is no real obligation for the higher-ups to consult the lower-downs nor is there any law which requires the former to take seriously any comments or suggestions made them by the latter. Indeed, the slightest recommendation or whisper of democracy is often looked upon as dissent, heresy, blasphemy!

Undeniably, the structures of most religions are both monarchic and male chauvinist, but there is no reason to assume that they are so by divine decree, It can be shown that these characteristics emerged because of historical accident: they happened to be the dominant ones in the then socio-political set-up at the time these religions emerged. Quite understandably – and uncritically! – these qualities were taken over into the nascent religious structures. But there is no need to stick stubbornly to them in today's democratic world, where many "laity" are far more knowledgeable than the clergy (which was not the case some centuries ago), where women are beginning to make their voices heard and the value of pluralism and de-centralisation is being appreciated. Religious authorities must become aware of how much religion has suffered by its leaders refusing to listen. If they do not "tune in" to the new voices and merging trends in today's world – albeit critically – they may find themselves ignored, in turn, by contemporary seriously religious-minded people.

"Dictators ride to and fro upon tigers, which they dare not dismount. And the tigers are getting hungry." –Winston Churchill

"I don't mind how much my ministers talk – so long as they do what I say!" –Margaret Thatcher

"As for being a General, well, at the age of four with paper hats and wooden swords, we're all Generals. Only some of us never grow out of it!" –Peter Ustinov

Appendix to Chapter 5

ELEMENTARY COMPARATIVE RELIGION

Introduction

Nowadays, for the first time, religious pluralism is becoming a fact in Europe and the USA. Though many of the first scholars of Comparative Religion had been Europeans, notably Nordics, in whose homelands this discipline originated at the turn of the century, the fact is that religious pluralism was the object of study in the West, whereas in Asia it was something lived and experienced in one's daily life. For centuries, Asians have lived side by side with people of other religious persuasions in peace and harmony, built up firm friendships with them and even inter-married. The phenomenon of inter-religious unrest and rioting is a very recent development in Asia. Indeed, it has been argued that it was first encouraged and provoked by the colonial powers who saw this as a means to consolidate their precarious hold over so vast a population, as per the tried and tested "divide and rule" formula! More recently, unscrupulous political leaders have found it a useful way to seize power through "religious vote banks"!

a. Gnostic vs Agapeic Religions

Aloysius Pieris, the eminent Sri Lankan Jesuit scholar, has lived out a deep religious and humanistic dialogue with his Buddhist countrymen. He has drawn attention to the often simplistic polarisations of religions, East and West, that students of comparative religions have often made. One of his concerns, the naive opposition between what has been called gnostic (from the Greek, gnosis, knowledge) and agapeic (Greek, agape. spiritual love) religions. Gnostic religions are those which stress wisdom or enlightenment as the way to salvation; agapeic religions, on the other hand, emphasise the way of service through active love. Among the gnostic religions can be ranked the religions born in India, such as Hinduism, Jainism and Buddhism. The "biblical religions", Judaism, Christianity and Islam, would be agapeic. But, as Pieris remarks, there can be no water-tight compartmentalisation of the two: love must meet wisdom. Indeed, *Love Meets Wisdom* is the title of one of his key studies on this issue. It is the fruit of many years of a dialogue of life and shared religious experience between Christian and Buddhist monks and nuns in his native land. He observes:

> Gnosis is salvific knowledge and agape is redemptive love. They are not soteriological [i.e. having to do with salvation] alternatives or optional paths to human liberation. They are two mystical moods that alternate according to the spiritual fluctuation of individuals, groups and even of entire cultures, without either of them allowing itself to be totally submerged by the other. Nor can they mix to form a hybrid or a "synthesis", for "never the twain shall meet", as Kipling would insist. They are, in other words, two irreducibly distinct languages of the spirit, each incapable, unless aided and complemented by the other, of mediating and adequately expressing the human encounter with the ultimate. Any valid spirituality, Christian or otherwise, must and, as history shows, does retain both poles of religious experience. It is the dialectical interplay of wisdom and love that ensures a progressive movement in the realm of the human spirit.[23]

Love and Wisdom must meet. For, without wisdom or enlightenment, love can all too easily degenerate into fanaticism and, without love, wisdom can become little better than proud elitism. It is all too easy for one tradition to misrepresent the other with an inexcusable reductio ad absurdum, as Pieris observes. Indeed, there is quite an "honour roll" of "great generalisers" who have encouraged such a naive approach: "Teilhard de Chardin, S. Radhakrishnan, Carl Gustav Jung and even the otherwise cautious C. Zaehner."

Gnosticism is a bad word for Western Christianity: it carries the connotations of overweening pride in human capacities, a rejection of the need for divine grace in the human quest for the Absolute. For, as Pieris reminds us, once again, gnosticism is only known to Western Christians in one or other of its "heretical" variants, docetism, Manicheeism, Catharism. Albigensianism ... But authentic gnosticism is "the liberating doctrine of the saving Truth, dawning in a person already disposed toward its reception by a process of self-purification or renunciation." That is why Pieris will say, in effect, that Christianity must let itself be first evangelised by authentic non-Christian gnosis before it can speak to others about God's preferential love for the poor.

23 Pieris, Aloysius. *Love Meets Wisdom: A Christian Experience of Buddhism*. New Delhi, India: Intercultural Pub, 1996.

b. "Atheistic" Religions

Jainism and Buddhism are two heterodox movements which arose within Hindu India during the 6th century B. C. It is time to take a closer look at these two "atheistic" traditions in religion, to which we have already had occasion to make reference.

The success of Buddhism is well known. It flourished in India for over twelve centuries and almost died out in its native land until it was revived by Dr Ambedkar in his efforts to liberate his fellow "untouchables" from the caste yoke. Missionaries carried it to other Asian lands and now it has well and truly "inculturated" itself in Tibet, Sri Lanka, Burma (Myanmar), parts of Thailand, Indonesia and even Japan. It has numerous followers today in Europe and the U. S. Its founder, Gautama, the Buddha (Enlightened One), has often been described as. "Hinduism's Martin Luther" and, like that other religious reformer, rose in revolt against a corrupt priestcraft and, after attaining enlightenment, taught his followers a "middle path", avoiding extremes in asceticism and devotion, building up a deeply spiritual tradition of people who, without the help of priests or clergy would try to attain self-mastery (salvation) by control of the passions and desires. Self-control, not divine grace, was the great Buddhist means of self-realisations.

Jainism is India's other "atheistic religion". It is much less known. Though it never overwhelmed the country, it never seemed to relax its hold on a small minority of Indians (mainly in today's South Western state of Gujarat) and it hardly managed to find any foreign converts: Few are aware that Mahatma Gandhi was born into this faith and derived his ahimsa (non-violence) from it. In practice, however, Gandhiji was more a Hindu of the mystical "bhakti" tradition than a strict Jain.

Jainism comes from Jina (spiritual conqueror), just as Buddhism comes from Buddha (Enlightened One) and is associated with the name of Mahavira (Great Hero), a kshatriya prince of North Bihar, whose real name was Vardhamana. A wandering ascetic, much given to extremes of meditation and austerity, he was gradually purified and reached a state of illumination by the time he was 43, after thirteen long years of intense penance and asceticism. At the time of his death, he had gathered around him several thousand monks, not to mention other adherents and female ascetics. Jains regard him as the twenty-fourth of a long line of Tirthankaras or guides. Jainism is the religion of those who seek to liberate themselves from the weary cycle of rebirth by following the teachings of these guides, as systematised by Mahavira Jina.

For the Jains, the whole universe (even minerals and fire) throb with life. Hence, they stress *ahimsa* (no-killing) and make strenuous efforts to avoid extinguishing life in any form. All lives are seen as stages in a series of transmigrations, caused by one's *karma* (actions). The higher forms of life are closer to complete liberation (*moksha*), which is finally achieved when the *jiva* (living organism) has been cleansed of all karmic particles. Among the means to be employed in this, there is mental concentration" (*yoga*) avoidance of evil deeds and desires, etc. But Jainism lays great stress on austerities. In this struggle for liberation, humans fight alone: there is no God and divine grace to help. Following the path of the great role-models, the Tirthankaras, one must, by his/her own heroic effort seek to break the circle of rebirth and attain that perfect state (*nirvana*), characterised by the four infinities of infinite perception, knowledge, power and bliss.

Hinduism is a religion with no recognisable historical founder. It is assumed to have always existed, from the beginnings of time. Scholars distinguish between popular or "folk" Hinduism, as it is lived (and has been lived) for centuries by simple, often uneducated and illiterate rural people and the literary or "elite" Hinduism of the more scholarly and higher cultural traditions.

To most people, Hindus are polytheistic idolaters, but this is as gross a misrepresentation of the religion as it would be for someone to accuse Roman Catholics, with their multitude of statues of venerated holy man and women, of sharing in the same convictions! Authentic Hinduism is monotheistic, recognising but one sovereign Absolute (Brahman), with its several manifestations (required by human finite needs, not objective in themselves). Just about everyone knows of the Hindu doctrine of karma and rebirth. In its original form (as mirrored in the famous Purusa-Shukta myth in the Rig Veda) it was more likely meant to be a symbolic depiction of the inter-connectedness and inter-dependence of all beings. It was perhaps not meant to be taken literally and thus be seen as a kind of metaphysical basis for the caste system with its rigid rules and oppression of the so-called outcastes. It is a great pity that this Hindu version of St Paul's doctrine of the Mystical Body should have degenerated into something so divisive and hierarchical-ridden in the hands of a powerful and dominant clerical caste.

c. Cosmic and Tribal Religions

A common characteristic of all tribal religions is a sense of closeness to nature. Indeed, this has often led them to be hastily described as inculcating "nature worship" and a common adjective for them is "animistic". But closer study reveals that tribal religions accept some Supreme Deity, called various names in various countries and by different tribes. Often some natural object is revered as the closest visible symbol of the numinous – fire, the sun and so on. A deep sense of respect for the forest, rivers, mountains and all living things pervades tribal life. Tribals do not erect temples of places of worship. Instead they make use of a natural shrine – the sacred grove, or *sarna*. as it is called in India. Tribals tend to have a very close-knit social set-up: everyone feels responsible for everyone else and the poor, orphans, widows and the ages are taken care of, very lovingly, by the whole community. Besides the Great Spirit, tribals recognise a host of inferior spirits who dwell in natural elements. Many of these are seen to be malefic and a good deal of tribal religious activity is preoccupied with trying to ward off their curses or harmful intents. Thus, a good deal of fear fills the life of a tribal. Tribal religious festivals are bound up with the evolution of the seasons and the various stages of agricultural life. The great challenge of tribal life today is to know where to draw the line between preserving their age-old culture and tradition and adapting these to the demands of our technological world. There is no easy solution and endless debates rage this way and that as to how far to go and how far to withdraw.

d. Bonhoeffer and "Non-Religious" Christianity

Dietrich Bonhoeffer (1909-1945) was a German theologian, a member of the courageous and outspoken Confessing Church, during the *ignominious* days of Nazi power. In 1945 he was arrested for his denunciation of national Socialism and his involvement in a conspiracy to overthrow Hitler. He was hanged in 1945, shortly before Germany fell to the allies.

In his controversial *Letters and Papers from Prison*, edited and published by his friend, the pastor Eberhard Bethge, he called for the establishment of a "religionless Christianity", one of his most hotly debated ideas. The traditional "religious a priori", upon which faith communities are customarily built is, according to him, a sense of hopelessness and inadequacy as regards the human person. This is taken as the basic ground for needing God.

Nowadays, however, as Bonhoeffer avers, "Man has learned to cope with all questions of importance without recourse to God as a working hypothesis." Nor did he mean this to be a kind of rueful and negative comment on the crass irreligiousness of modem man. It was to be seen, rather, as an indication that we have "come of age" in matters religious and require a more adult approach to God than the traditional childish path that dwelt upon human weakness, helplessness and insufficiency. Just as, in the past, religious leaders had to accommodate themselves to the fact that believers were no longer turning to God (and the clergy!) for aid in coping with problems related to health and the weather, but to doctors and the meterological department, being forced to admit that these were not the outcome of perverse human pride and irreligiosity, so also they must learn to accept the fact that we no longer need to rush to God when faced with the "ultimate questions" (death, guilt, etc.). It is a sad thing that most clergy only know how to make God relevant to their contemporaries when the latter are at the end of their tether, in a "limit situation". He feels it would be far better to teach man to live bravely without answers to the so-called' "ultimate questions", rather than use these to break down the last vestiges of his courage and self-confidence. There seems to be something utterly ignoble in the strategy of falling upon "unhappy people in their worst moment (to) force upon them a sort of religious conversion", when they are too broken and dispirited to resist, as at the moment of some shattering personal tragedy, like the death of a loved one.

So, in place of the long-standing traditionally "religious" interpretation of the human condition, Bonhoeffer offers a more relevant "wordly interpretation" This implies living *etsi Deus non daretur* (i.e. as if there were no God: note, the use of the Latin subjunctive implies that Bonhoeffer does believe in God). In other words, we must "live before God as if there were no God." This means that we must live consciously in the embrace of God's empowering love and grace ("living before God"), but we should not expect miracles and revelations to come our way and make things easier for us (as if there were no God"). This is what Bonhoeffer would call the authentic Christian attitude. Can we extend this challenge to all religions, to any authentic religion, any religion that would be worthy of its name in our contemporary world? Too often has religion led people to shun their responsibilities, childishly dumping their responsibilities on God's lap, instead of taking them and their lives into their own hands, like adults!

"If the concept of God has any validity or use, it can only be to make us larger, freer and more loving. If God cannot do this, then it is time we got rid of him." –James Baldwin

"Science without religion is law, religion without science is blind." –Albert Einstein

"To become a popular religion, it is only necessary for a superstition to enslave a philosophy." –Dean Inge

"So many gods, so many creeds, So many paths that wind and wind, While just the art of being kind Is all the sad world needs." –Elsa Wheeler Cox

Chapter 6

CREATION. EVOLUTION. EMANATION

Introduction

At first sight, this chapter promises to be a purely academic issue – a per - haps(?) interesting, but not very relevant comparative study of the various ways in which humans have sought to explain the origin of the universe. But a little serious reflection should make us realise that this is actually a very practical issue and has a lot to do with "the ordinary business of living". It raises points which are of significance, not just for philosophers and theologians, but for the man and woman in the street.

For this chapter is about origins and "origins are normative". In other words, how a things begins (or how we conceive of its beginning) has a lot to do with what it is meant to be (or, once again, what we conceive it is meant to be). In other words, our convictions about how the world began will have an impact on how we see ourselves "fitting into it", how seriously we should take it, how active we should be in it and for what purpose!

Most people, of course, are quite unaware as to how their basic concepts and ideas do influence – and often prejudice – their attitudes and actions with regard to everything else. It would, thus, be worth our while to spend some time on matters like this.

And straightaway we note that the earliest human speculations about the origin and nature of the world are "shrouded in myth". As we have already reflected on the significance and relevance of myth, even in our technological set-up, there is no need to issue caveats about taking a too indulgent and patronising attitude to these ancient insights. As we may recall, all views about the origin of the world – whether put in the language of science, philosophy or theology – assume their most personal significance when recast in the poetic language of myth.

Of course, we will not be able to go into a detailed study of the vast and rich inventory of the world's myths about the origin of things. That would take too much time and is, in any case, far beyond the capacity of the present writer. We will confine our study to the Adamic myth of origins: it is taken seriously by three great world religions and is well known. Nor will it be our concern, here, to "prove" (or attempt to prove) which of the three historical approaches to cosmogenesis is correct. Our main concern will be to study the implications and assumptions of each of the three, with a view to figuring out which gives us the most dynamic vision of reality and which would provide us with a blue-print for action for liberation. As far as I am concerned, "evolution" has a well-established scientific basis. I will endeavour to show that it neither contradicts creation (properly understood), nor does the biblical account of "creation" in Genesis contradict it. Even if I do not accept "emanation" I recognise an important truth, often overlooked, that it points towards.

1. Creation

a. The Adam and Eve Story

To begin with, the word "creation" isn't to be found in any of the two accounts of creation in the Hebrew Bible (Chs. 1 and 2 of Genesis). This is true, even though most translations begin, "In the beginning, God created the heavens and the earth..." This is not because Genesis denies the fact of creation, much less refuses to believe that God can create; it is simply due to the fact that the ancient Jews (like the ancient Greeks) had no word in their vocabulary of the time for "nothingness", or "zero". Now, as everyone knows, the characteristic of creation is that it is a "making out of nothing" (i.e. no pre-existing raw material). Thus, Genesis sees God rather as "fashioning" the world (Hebrew, *bara*) Indeed, the nearest the ancients could get to the idea of "nothingness" was the Hebrew *tohu wabohu* which had the same meaning as the Greek word, chaos (whose form and meaning we have taken bodily into English). In other words, Genesis (believe it or not!) does not see God so much as creating the world out of nothing but as bringing an orderly world out of primeval chaos and confusion. Once again, let me stress that it's not that the ancients denied that God could make something out of nothing; they had no word for "nothing!"

(It was left to India to come out with this complex and insightful pseudo-concept: Sanskrit, *sunya*). The reason why it took us so long to realise all this was because it is only recently have believers in the Bible overcome (somewhat!) their anti-Semitic prejudices and listened to Jewish biblical scholars helping us to interpret the so-called "Old Testament"; let us not forget the fact that the entire Bible is a Jewish book and we cannot expect to understand its meaning and symbolism without a thorough knowledge of the Jewish ethos and culture of the time.

The first practical relevance of this "bringing order out of chaos" rather than "creating out of nothing" perspective is that it gives us an insight as to what human life is meant to be about. For, a little later (in Gen 1:26), we are told that humans are made "in God's image and likeness". Now this means that, according to the biblical vision creation is to bring order out of chaos, as God, our model or exemplar, has just been described as having done. The foundations what is called "liberation theology" are laid in the very first words of the Bible!

Apart from the fact that Genesis doesn't uphold creation (at least not explicitly, though creation – in the technical sense – may be implied in it), we can say that the entire question of the origin of the world is not the purpose of the Adamic myth at all. Genesis is using the literary form of a genealogy to give us some important truths, couched in symbolic language. But we need to interpret the story, not seek its message in the literal sense.

To make a long story short, a genealogy, as a literary form, was commonly used by the ancient Hebrews to tell us something about the nature and purpose of a thing or what a particular person's role in life was supposed to be, from the perspective of God. This can be seen exemplified by the two genealogies of Jesus in the New Testament (Mt 1:1-17 and Lk 3:23-37). Taken literally, these two lists flatly contradict each other. On closer scrutiny, we note that they are highly selective and with a purpose. Each, by stressing different ancestors of the Messiah, highlight aspects of his mission that have a special relevance for the believing communities they were primarily addressed to.

Now, just as these genealogies of Jesus were more interested in telling us who he was than giving us an exact historical picture of those by whom he came to be, so is it with the genealogies in Genesis: the genealogies of the World, of Man (Adam), Woman (Eve) and sin. These are not – repeat not! – interested in telling us how they came into being (their origin), but rather what they are (their nature and destiny). Thus, we are told, as regards the World, that everything in it is good, as against the current Manichaeistic idea that anything material was evil, the production of a rival evil deity. Furthermore, we are told, in effect, that all we see around us is not God: it was made by God, so is not to be worshipped. That is why, for example, we are told that God created light even before the Sun and Moon were called into being. The message is clear: God is the author of light, so essential for life. The Sun, whom many at the time adored as God, is not the real source of light.

In the second creation story (chapter 2 of Genesis) the focus of attention shifts to the Nature and Destiny of the Human Person: What is Man? He is earthy (fashioned by God from "the slime of the earth"), yet divine (God's breath or life is in him). And what is Woman? The story of God making Eve out of Adam's rib is not meant to be taken as a statement that men have one rib less than women (which they do not): it is to be read and interpreted as a symbol. Woman is not made out of some inferior part of man (his foot, say) but from that, which is nearest to his heart: she is to be loved and cherished, held close to his heart as his equal. Furthermore, she is no mere member of the "weaker sex": as "rib" she protects the heart and so, in some cases, it is woman who is the stronger sex, protecting man from harm. In fact, the biblical lesson is clear enough: Man and Woman have complementary strengths, each supporting the other in different contexts! Let us also note, in passing, that the story of the Serpent and the Forbidden Fruit has nothing to do with how sin began ("original sin") but is a cautionary tale to illustrate what sin is and what its consequences are (divisiveness between Man and Woman as also between Humans and Nature, sin is foolish, unnecessary etc).

b. Philosophising about "Creation"

The popular understanding of creation as "making something out of nothing" traces its roots back to the more sophisticated and technical definition first elaborated by St Augustine of Hippo (354-430). The original Latin of his words is a bit difficult to translate, "*productio rei ex nihilo sui et subjecti.*" A free translation would be something like, "Creation is the production of something real, out of no pre-existing raw material, nor out of anything from the creative cause." The definition has three parts. Let us examine each separately:

1. *It is the making of something real:* What is made or brought into existence, the act of creation, is something existentially real. It is not of the ideal order. It is something radically new, that wasn't there before. So, it is not a mere question of discovering something that had been there all along, but hidden or unobserved.

2. *No pre-existing raw material:* We have already touched on the implications of this when explaining total dependence. Suffice is it to recall for now that God, in creation, did not fashion something out of pre-existing wood or metal, as would a carpenter. However, there is one more misunderstanding to clear up. This concerns the simplistic way some people have understood the phrase "making something out of nothing." This "nothing" must not be understood as a kind of raw material out of which God fashions things, like the proverbial carpenter, making his table "out of wood"! It merely means that something totally and radically new has come to be and nothing in it was existing, before the act of creation. A misunderstanding of this clause in the definition has resulted in all those negative ontologies who see "nothing" as in-built into the constitution of reality, just as wood is inbuilt into the wooden table !

3. *Not made out of something in the creative cause:* Authentic creation cancels out any raw material outside of, or external to, the creative cause (cf no 2, above). It also rules out the created thing as being made out of some raw material taken from within the creative cause, as when a spider spins a web out

of no external raw material, but out of its insides, as it were. It is this last part of the definition that distinguishes creation from emanation, about which we will say more in due time.

Comment: We have lined up a useful enough definition of "creation". It throws sufficient light on the issue to rule out the more common misunderstandings and is a useful enough pointer to what we're talking about when we use the term. However, it is a mere *negative definition*: it focuses more on what creation is not, than on what it is (it is not making out of raw materials, it is not making out of something flowing from the creative cause). Is it possible to give a more positive definition? Again, St Augustine's definition tells us what creation is from the point of view of the effect (i.e. the creature). What is creation from the point of view of the cause (i.e. creator)? The answer to both these questions is, "Creation is total ontological dependence."

One of the reasons why we find it so hard to grasp what creation implies is the fact that we are quite unable to visualise or imagine what it's like. And this is because "we are unable to make anything in such a way that it is totally ontologically dependent" on us. Now total ontological dependence means all-round dependence for a thing's existence. In other words, the thing concerned is dependent on its cause for every aspect of its existence – for its coming-to-be (its genesis or origin), its staying in being, its raw materials, its activities (for activities are a kind of "being", too): everything!

Nor does it mean that ontological dependence, in this case, makes a mockery of human freedom. True, our activities depend ontologically on God for their existence as being. But their specification – whether the activity be one of building up or pulling down, of loving or hating – that depends on me. To understand this better, think of the electric power available for our use at home. The generating station supplies the power: it's up to me to decide whether I use it to iron clothes, cook my food or watch my favourite TV programme (or do all these simultaneously). The *specification* is up to me.

What we've just said about creation being total ontological dependence should also make it easier for us to understand another somewhat complex issue in this regard and that is the notion of an eternal creation. As long as we define creation negatively, it's difficult to see that there is no contradiction in the idea of an eternal creation. But if we understand creation in the more positive way, it's easier to grasp that "eternal creation" is not something like a "square circle" – a flat contradiction. That there be an eternal ontological dependence is easier to; grant than an eternal making (the verbal form misleads us into thinking of an activity that occurs suddenly in time). After all, God is not obliged to, create at all: God is free to do so or not. And, if God decides to create, there is no obligation, once again, that this be in time or eternal. It's up to God to choose. If God chose to create in eternity (which means outside of what, we normally call time) then there would never be a moment when the universe (in some form or other) was not! Nor would this make creation indistinguishable from God. God would be existing from all eternity and in total independence from any other being. The universe (in whatever form) would be "always there", side-by-side with God (to use an inaccurate human-image), but would be there while totally depending on God.

But was our world and the universe created in time or from eternity? The only one who could answer that question definitively is God. And to the best of my knowledge, we have received no such information from God. No holy book – certainly not the Bible – says anything definitive on the topic. What about the positive sciences? Can they throw any light on the matter? Well, there is the phenomenon of entropy, spoken of in thermodynamics. It seems to indicate that the world *does* have a beginning in time, i.e., is not eternal. In brief, it has been observed that the various forms of energy in the cosmos are gradually being converted into less and less useful forms. This would imply that the universe will eventually (after zillions of years?) reach what is known as the stage of heat-death, that is a condition when the useful energy available in the universe would be zero. Now, it is argued, if this "running down" has been going on from eternity, assuredly, the whole thing would have "run down" by now and the heat-death stage would already have been upon us. But this is obviously not the case. So ... Whatever one thinks of this argument, one thing is clear: only scientists would be able to tell us whether the world had a beginning in time or not.

2. Evolution

a. No Necessarily Excludes Creation

The notion of evolution does not necessarily contradict the idea of creation. In fact, it would seem that evolution presupposes creation. Whatever it is that evolved, a primordial protoplasmic globule or the super-molecule which started the whole ball rolling with a "big bang", one is quite justified in asking where that limited being, which cannot explain its origin, came from. God, then, would not be envisaged as having created finished products but a dynamically evolving cosmos, an evolutionary universe. This calls for a bit of further precision in our terminology.

Creationism: This view certainly contradicts the whole idea of evolution. It refers to the conviction of some fundamentalist Christians and others that the book of Genesis (like every other book in the Bible, according to them) must be taken literally. Hence, God is seen as having created the world, day by day, as a series of completed, finished products. Such an interpretation of Scripture, of course, rules out any possibility of evolution. Most believers in the Bible, however, uphold a view of creation, which sees God as having created, as we have mentioned above, that super-molecule or whatever, that gradually evolved, over millions of years, into the cosmos as we have it today. Such people subscribe to creation, but aren't "creationists"!

Evolutionism: This view is a development of Darwin, who had a rather limited view as to what evolved. Evolutionism holds that everything, from the distantest galaxies to the entire human person evolved from a primitive super-molecule. This is, by no means, a necessarily irreligious and atheistic position, as we shall see.

Transformism: This is a kind of concessional view of evolution and, indeed, Darwin's doctrine was a kind of transformism. It limits the evolutionary process to living beings only and excludes any human evolution from the process because of a particular conception of the human soul. Thus, we have universal transformism which upholds the passage from one primitive cell to the human body (but not "the soul: that is held to be created separately by God either at, or some time after, conception) and then there is mitigated transformism which restricts itself to an acceptance of a separate development of each species by itself.

b. Why Evolution Was Opposed by Believers

Evolutionism was opposed by religious believers (especially Christians) because, apart from the fact that it contradicted a literal interpretation of Genesis it seemed to both degrade the human person and water down God's creative power. Humans are no longer the summit of creation, as the Bible seemed to have taught, but a mere slightly evolved brute animal, only accidentally (not essentially) different from apes and dolphins. Furthermore, it appears to detract from the primary and unique causality of God, assigning to other beings some kind of active role in the process of cosmogenesis.

As to the first charge it can be shown that an evolutionary vision of the cosmos and of the origin of the humans actually enhances our personal dignity and responsibility all the more. The *Weltanschauung* of Pierre Teilhard de Chardin SJ (1881-1955) is illustrative of this possibility. I am not saying that his vision is the only way of exemplifying this, nor even necessarily the best way. I am just high-lighting it to show that religious faith and a conviction concerning evolution can go together and involve no necessary compromises about human dignity or God's creative power. Teilhard sees the evolutionary process as unfolding in two stages. The first stage occurs by way of unconscious forces, from the big bang, climaxing in the eventual emergence of the human person (via all kinds of fits and starts and digressions). The goal of this initial stage is *hominisation* (the human person is the goal of the whole striving). Then comes the second stage, in which we recognise that "Man is evolution become conscious of itself." Now the further movement of evolution must be deliberately sought as the result of a conscious decision on our part. Whereas, in the first phase, evolution was characterised by dispersion, multiplicity and variety ("radial energy"), it is "tangential energy" that should dominate in the next: the human person must ensure a movement of recapitualation, of drawing together, of reintegrating. This is to be done through the development of science and technology as much as by advances in human spiritual enlightenment. Whatever, in a far more striking and dynamic manner than in the pre-evolutionary understanding, the human plays a central role.

As for the role of God in the whole process, Teilhard's vision is one that high-lights the divine wisdom and power all the more. Instead of God acting again and again in history (very much like we do), getting each finished product started and then intervening every time a human soul is supposed to come into existence, we have God packing into the primitive super-molecule all the force and energy that it would require to eventually evolve the cosmos with all its complex denizens. God is the infinitely far-seeing and wise choreographer of a vast cosmic ballet which, slowly but surely climaxes towards the emergence of the human person, equipped with freedom, and who is given scope to play a real responsible role, along with God, in the whole dance! God emerges far more clearly in this perspective as an infinitely wise master-planner, who yet values freedom and assigns to each creature as much scope for spontaneity, initiative and freedom it is capable of. Nor is the human person given such a crucial role because God *had* to, but, rather, because God *wanted* to!

3. Emanation

This word has an ancient and glorious lineage and traces its roots all the way from Indian and Egyptian mythology to Neoplatonism and Christian Gnosticism and beyond. The Greek equivalent is *aporroia*, *probole* or *pro-odos* and the Latin term is *emanatio*. All these imply a kind of "flowing-forth", comparable to efflux or radiation. Emanationist cosmogenesis speaks of the origin of reality by way of an "overflow" or "issuing forth" from the transcendent first cause (God). Emanation is described as "timeless" and so cannot strictly be qualified as a "process". It is supposed to leave its source "undiminished" as fire "emanates" heat, snow "emanates" a spider "emanates" cold and its web. However, as emanation-unfolds, each successive product becomes less perfect than its predecessor. Emanation now has a clearly pantheistic connotation, though it did not always have.

The chief difference between emanation and evolution lies in the fact that the former implies a continuous degradation and the latter continuous growth in perfection. If some early conceptions of evolution did not go against the transcendence of the source, nowadays, as I have said, the pantheistic understanding of it is inevitable. This pantheistic connotation seems to be the result of two fairly distinct motives, one more mystical, the other more metaphysical. The mystical strain in all of us inclines us to a holistic vision of reality, one which sees all things as interdependent and interconnected (as present-day ecological concerns have confirmed): "Each time you move your little finger, you rock the furthest star ," says the poet! And, as we have seen, God is immanent in all reality, inasmuch as there is an intimate, unbreakable bond between God and creatures. Now it is all too easy to exaggerate this truth, forget transcendence, and end up in a total identification of the creator and the creature – pantheism!

The metaphysical roots of the pantheistic understanding of things arise if one does not have an evolved vocabulary of analogy to fall back upon. If one espouses an equivocal understanding of being and, furthermore, so defines it as to make it possible that only God can be called "being", then the only way to save the reality of ourselves and all that surrounds us is to end up identifying it all with God, who alone is "being"! This was the approach of the Indian sage, Ramanuja, who wanted to "save the reality of the external world." On the other hand, there was Sankara who, anxious to maintain the transcendence of the Absolute, opted for the non-being (*maya*) condition of reality!

Pantheism presents lots of problems and contradictions that have to be resolved. First, if everything is ultimately and fundamentally one with God, how do we explain the fact of wickedness and evil? If these are real – and it's very difficult, if not impossible to hold otherwise — then they must be identified with God, somehow! Next, the existence of the World/Universe ends as somehow or the other necessary for the Absolute which would otherwise be somehow "incomplete" without creation! Some "emanationists" try to evade this impasse by postulating an "eternal emanation". But merely "pushing back" emanation into eternity doesn't really solve the problem: it still becomes necessary for the Absolute's fullness that it emanate! Finally, there is the problem of salvaging human freedom, initiative and spontaneity from the whole process. In pantheism, it is invariably the Absolute who controls and makes all things happen. It seems to me that emanation is not a very liberative understanding of reality!

"God made everything out of nothing, but the nothingness shows through."
–Paul Valéry

"Descended from the apes? My dear, we will hope it is not true. But if it is, let us pray that it may not become generally known."
–Wife of an English cleric

"I asserted – and I repeat — that a man has no reason to be ashamed of having an ape for his grandfather. If there were an ancestor whom I should feel shame in recalling, it would rather be a man ...!
–Thomas Huxley

Chapter 7

PROVIDENCE AND FREEDOM

a. Introductory Notions

How do we understand Divine Providence (the belief that just about all religions share, that God is "taking care of" the world and each of us, especially) in such a way that human freedom doesn't become an empty word? If everything that happens in the world is part of some "vast cosmic plan" – and this is what Divine Providence means to many of us – then where does human initiative and free choice come in? As the devoutly Catholic French thinker, Maurice Blondel (1861-1949) put it, "If the history of human thought and action unfolds according to some pre-established plan, if the whole of it has already been thought out – not to say 'written out' – by God, then it loses its human import."

My purpose here is not, first of all, to "prove" that thesis such a thing as human freedom. That is something we can take as a "given" from another branch of philosophy, correcting naive and simplistic understandings of it, from the data of behavioural psychology and psychoanalysis. For the time being, let us merely note that if we are not in any way free at all, then the whole system of rewards and punishments, of law courts and jurisprudence, as veil as of gallantry awards would have no meaning. Nor would I have any justification to scold a child who stole jam or prosecute someone who robbed me of my life savings or raped my sister! I am quite sure no one would want a society based on such implications.

b. Relevance of the Problem

Apart from trying to find a way to harmonise one's understanding of Divine Providence with one's convictions about human freedom, there are other ticklish Issues that equally deserve our attention. There is the whole area of prayer of petition. Granted that we should not identify prayer exclusively with that, the question still remains: what is the role, if any, of prayer of petition in the life of the believer? If we really are free and have some meaningful responsibility in this world, wouldn't it be better to get down to action, rather than pray when confronted with some need or problem? And, if there is such a thing as Divine Providence, if God is taking care of things, why should we waste time asking him to do what he is doing already? And if God has fore-ordained everything (which is what Divine Providence seems to entail) what's the point of asking him to revise his plans?

We hear a lot about "God's will" and his "divine plan" in sermons and at funerals. We meet people who tell us how their prayers were heard and how they or someone they knew was "miraculously healed" or saved from some impending disaster. But, on the other hands, there seem to be as many (or even more!) people – including ourselves? – who have had contrary experiences with prayers apparently unanswered, no miraculous healing in a situation equally meritorious or urgent. To many, it seems that there are but a "privileged few" whose prayers and faith are rewarded and nothing that others do seems to win them a rank among these. To make matters worse, the bad people seem to be prospering (witness the corrupt politicians, shady business folk and mafia bosses while the decent, honest and fair-minded people are left out in the cold. What sort of providence is this if it can't stand by those who try to live by decent human values or support innocent widows, orphans and deprived poor people against the ravages of those who spurn all laws and boldly proclaim that they "fear neither God nor the devil"!

Of course, there have been wise (and otherwise!) attempts to respond to all such difficulties, but many of these do more credit to people's hearts than their heads. St Augustine tried to explain why many of our prayers seem to go unanswered: it's all due to one or more of three possible reasons, "We are evil people, we ask for evil things and we ask in an evil way." But, if God loves all people unconditionally (as St Augustine himself avers), then why would he disregard the prayer of the sinner or the one who didn't say his/ her prayers well? Isn't that "making conditions"? The only explanation that can still stand is the middle one: we had, unknowingly, asked God for something which wouldn't have been good for us. But surely God could have helped us to make proper use of that thing? Besides, we have many instances when people have, apparently, been allowed to have things which they would later make bad use of!... As for the evil prospering and the good faring badly, I remember being told that God was' merely rewarding the "baddies" for the little good they had managed to do in this world (they'd get their just desserts after death, was the implication). And don't worry about bad things happening to good people: they're assured of heaven when they die (shades of Marx's religion-opium equation)!

c. The Basis of Divine Providence

Many of the difficulties that people have with Divine Providence stem from the fact that they are still operating within a static vision of reality. However, things look different when we view reality from a dynamic perspective!

Now one of the most revolutionary insights in recent years is our passage from a static to a dynamic conception of reality. Indeed, it seems clear enough to anyone who has eyes to see, that ours is definitely not a "finished product" world, but one that is still "in the making". God's creative evolution is an ongoing process and that process is unfolding right now. Seeds are growing into plants, bushes and trees. Poems and novels are being written. Animal and human foetuses are growing, clumsily learning to make sounds and walk.

Now, if ours is really a dynamic world, a world "in the making" as we have said and not a "finished product world", then Divine Providence would basically consist of the fact of God's having "provided" each reality with the inner dynamism (laws of nature) to orient and guide them to the full flowering and development of their being. Sub-human things, as well as humans, have been "provided" with various physical, chemical, biological and so on laws or inbuilt mechanisms that non-consciously direct them to grow into what they are meant to be. These "inner laws" guide an acorn to develop into an oak tree and not a full-grown bull dog, just as the relevant proper laws "automatically" make a bull-dog pup eventually become a bull-dog and not an oak tree! All this is done non-consciously. We grow from infancy to childhood to adolescence and puberty up to adulthood, not as the result of deliberate decisions on our part. It "just happens" whether we will it or not.

In addition, humans are further provided with "freedom". This is because "becoming human" involves a bit more complexity than, say, "becoming a grown bulldog" or a "full-blossoming tree". A person might be quite manly, with a well - developed physique, plus "film-star features" to boot, but still be very in-human or impersonal. That is because authentic humanness is also a question of (freely) choosing and living by certain values. That is why God "provides" us with freedom, to enable us to become fully human, fully alive, over and above the provision of those internal dynamisms and biological laws that brings about our physical development and perfection. All this may be termed as making up "cosmic providence", all those inbuilt dynamisms that God has "provided" the cosmic super-molecule to enable it to finally develop into the myriad galaxies as well as all that would come to be on each planet or star. All this is what Teilhard de Chardin was referring to when he spoke of the first stage (or phase) of evolution, "radial energy".

Now, granting that the first phase was ultimately geared to "hominisation" or "the emergence of the human person" and, admitting that this was carried forward by deterministic non-conscious processes, we note that, as the data of

Paleontology makes it abundantly clear, this did not involve a planning down to the last detail. If the goal had been set, it was left for the strivings of matter through various false starts and colliding interaction and adaptations, to find Its way there. There was plenty of scope for chance and it is evident enough that the human person did not arrive on the scene by the shortest possible evolutionary route! Pierre Lecomte du Noüy coined the term "tele-finality" to describe this "direction from afar." God's cosmic providence did not involve him running alongside the process, as it were, giving it a push here and a nudge there. Nor did he map out everything like a clever computer programmer and then sat back, apparently, to watch the whole show unfolding along swift and efficient lines. As we said earlier, God set the goal (viz. hominisation), but let the evolutionary process find its way there by trial and error, something like the rain water pouring in torrents on a mountain top must find its way eventually to the bottom (Lecomte du Noüy's own illustrative example). And, as we have said, once the human person arrives on the scene, then we have to freely decide to carry on the evolutionary plan of God, integrating all things, gathering everything together in tangential energy. In other words, the human agent must freely assume (or reject) a key and decisive role in God's providential plan. We become active participators in the process of divine providence and, in a very real sense, God depends on us to attain the goals of divine providence that God was not obliged to do! God freely chose to make divine providence depend on our collaboration at this final evolutionary phase.

d. Personal Providence

We have spoken, so far, about cosmic providence – how God "provides" for the cosmos in general and each and every being within it. But, isn't there something like "personal providence", a kind of special divine care and guidance for persons, humans, as our various religions, generally speaking, teach or imply? This is the question we must investigate next.

Does personal providence mean that God has pre-determined our deaths? Many people, particularly religious believers think so. Very often, at funerals we hear people lamenting how God has "snatched away" a loved one from the bereaved family. People ask, "Why did God do this to us? Why did God take away my child/parent/spouse when I need him/her so much?" Others seek to console the mourning near and dear ones, saying, "God knows best. God took him/ her away now because it's better this way." Some people even derive some comfort and consolation from this kind of explanation. But let us ask ourselves why it is that we die at all, in the first place? Is it because God intervenes and "cuts off" our life supply?

We die for the same reason that iron rusts, that mountains erode and rivers dry up – all that is made up of matter must eventually fall apart into its material components. This can happen in one of two ways: either by the sudden irruption of some external agency, as when a virus or whatever enters our body and causes irreparable internal harm, or because something internal misfunctions (the heart "pump" breaks down or that mysterious thing we call, for want of a better word, "old age", sets in. The fact that we are embodied, material, implies that death is inbuilt into our very structure. Of course, we can well ask (and we will, in the next chapter) why God made us embodied at all, for were we not material we would not perish, as we wouldn't have material parts to fall back into. There is no need to postulate any kind of God of death who would pre-determine the precise time, place and means of our death, from which there'd be no escape when that inexorable moment comes. Of course, as we shall see in a moment, God does fore-know our deaths, as indeed God fore-knows all that has yet to come about, but divine fore-knowledge does not in any way imply pre-determination. We'll come to that later!

Does God make things happen so that others can learn a lesson? Once again, many pious believers are quite convinced of this and, indeed, they often find meaning or comfort in times of tragic mishaps by falling back on such an explanation. A young boy is killed in a motor accident, leaving behind his old parents, shattered and broken. "Why didn't you take me and spare my son?" cries the lad's distraught mother. Someone tries to console her saying that God, in effect, "used" the death of this boy to teach others that they should be more careful on the road, or to prevent him from doing some bad deed in his later life. When a young couple are shocked to find that their firstborn child is physically deformed or mentally retarded, priests tell them that God made the child so, in order that the parents learn to become more selfless and learn to grow in love, etc. And some people manage to find some "meaning" thereby in this suffering.

But what is the basis of speaking like this? There is nothing in any Holy Book I know of to warrant it – certainly not in the Bible. Furthermore, it seems to me that, were God to resort to such a gruesome pedagogy, this would involve using persons as a means and this is evil, sinful (as even Kant recognised). God does not – cannot – do evil. And surely God is imaginative enough so as to find a better way to communicate salutary messages to us than by falling back on such ghoulish methodology! If God is anything worth paying attention to, God is a God of life, not death! If when sorrow and pain come our way, it is not expressly willed by God. God's intervention would be more on the lines of sending the doctor than the disease. But whence come all these unpleasant experiences, if not at the express will of God? My answer is that they come through the inter-play of secondary causes which often clash with each other within the relative autonomy granted to them by God – and not because God made them so interact. More about this in the last chapter.

So, what does personal providence involve? I've explained what is meant by "cosmic providence: God's provision, through the various laws and inner dynamisms of that natural guidance that directs creatures to their full growth and development. I've also explained what, as far as I am concerned, "personal providence" does *not* involve: it does not involve God's personal intervention to cause us to die, nor even some kind of remote pre-determination of the date, time and place (even though God fore-knows that: more about this, later). Nor does it imply God using persons merely as a means so that, through some tragic event, others may learn some salutary lesson! But what *does* personal providence positively involve? In the first place, it entails God's providential activity with individual persons, dialoguing with them in the depth of their hearts, through their experiences of prayer and through the various Holy Books and acts of worship they, as believing individuals, participate in. God also is involved, in similar ways, with unbelievers, too (for God is unconditional in love), speaking to them in their hearts, as well. God also calls to us through the events of secular and everyday history, inspiring us to action for justice (but leaving us free to respond positively or not to this interpellation).

The "fore-knowledge = pre-determination" fallacy: Our human way of knowing is dependent on objects. Hence, the only time we can accurately "predict" what is going to happen (foreknowledge) – apart from lucky guesses and stray "intuitions" (?) – are when we are somehow or the other, directly or indirectly, instrumental in making such things happen (pre-determination). If I can say with assurance that my neighbour's windows will be smashed at 10 p.m. tonight, it is because I've either arranged for them to be broken or am partly responsible for making it happen, in that I know of someone who has arranged for it to happen and, by keeping quiet about it as somehow an accessory. From this we make the hasty implicit argumentation that, in the same way, if God is able to fore-know something, then God must have pre-determined it!

The fallacy arises out of the assumption that God's way of knowing is exactly like ours and is also dependent on objects. But, if our way of knowing is dependent on outside reality and we can only come to know ourselves by knowing objects, with God it is just the opposite. God is pure spirit and so is able to know himself/herself perfectly and directly. Now, all that exists and all that can be is but a participation in God (is partly what God is fully). Thus, by knowing himself/herself, God knows all beings, for they are naught but participations in God. It doesn't matter whether the beings in question are actually existing or actually will exist later or remain at the "pure possibility" stage and never come to be. God knows them all by knowing himself/herself. God doesn't have to wait for things to be: he/she knows all beforehand (fore-knowledge) but this doesn't imply any interference or predetermination from God's part! God's way of knowing is diametrically opposite to ours. We know the world first and, by knowing the world, cope to know ourselves. God knows himself/herself exhaustively and directly and, by knowing himself/herself, knows all actual and possible creatures.

What about "miracles"? A lot depends on how we view miracles. If we view them as mere physical events, devoid of all religious connotation and interpret them to be a mere breach of the natural law, then this would hardly make any sense: such an interpretation makes a mockery of the whole concept of natural law. But if we alter our presupposition a bit and see things from a religious perspective, a miracle would be a significant event that strikingly mediates the presence of the immanent God, then everything takes on a different hue. The miracle would not be seen as in conflict with the natural law, which might have to be revised a bit to cover this apparent exception. Nor would every miraculous event have to be something of that stamp. It could be any inexplicable or coincidental experience that would be a powerful expression of God's love or care, a kind of "anticipatory sign" of God's kingdom. If traditional apologetics gave importance to miracle as seeing them as a means to compel faith, now we tend to see them as presupposing it. In other words, miracles would be more meaningful to those who belong to the community of faith (confirming and strengthening a faith already there), rather than being an effective means to convert the unbeliever!

e. Prayer is Not Just Petition Making

Let me, first of all, repeat that it is totally wrong to identify prayer with asking for things (even though the very word, prayer, seems to imply that). Indeed, it is because of this hasty over-generalisation that most people's prayer life never goes very deep and their relationship with God is superficial (theirs is a "super-market God"!). We could find an insight into authentic prayer by reflecting on our experience of a deep conversation with a close friend. How much of such exchanges are restricted to the "gimme" type of themes (give me this and give me that and do it right away, or else...)? In fact, if a major part of such "chats" were of that nature, there'd be very little love or friendship between the two persons concerned! What, actually, is the main topic of conversation between true friends or lovers? Isn't it rather expressions of love, trust and solidarity and sharings about all that happens to one, the momentous as much as the commonplace. There might be also "thank you", not so much for this or that service or favour rendered, but for the whole wonderful experience of the other's love. Occasionally there'd be an exchange concerned about forgiveness and reconciliation and, once in a while, a request for help. Sometimes, one may feel hurt or "let down" by a friend but, unless the whole relationship has been a very shallow, self- centred one, the friendship doesn't flounder and collapse because of that! I think there's a clue for us in all this, as regards our prayer life. And let us also recall the classical distinction between a person who prays and a person of prayer; the former denotes an action which one cannot do all the time, the latter points to an attitude. This attitude enables us to "find God in all things" (including a noisy marketplace and not just in solitude and mystic experience) because one has learnt to live before God (may we also add "as if there were no God", in the sense of Bonhoeffer?). And the most intense moments of "formal prayer" are the times when we are moved to lapse into loving, contemplative silence (true lovers can find a parallel in their own experience).

f. Prayer of Petition

It's not that we should never make prayers of petition (though, as we deepen our prayer-life, prayer of petition tends to decrease in proportion to other types of prayer). It's a question of getting our expectations concerning it into the proper perspective.

Isn't it a fact that the image of God that lies behind most of our prayers of petition is that of a technician or doctor who's far better than any human technician or doctor, a rival to them or, at best, to be invoked when human resource personnel fail or are unavailable. This would imply that as science and technology advance and as socio-economic development make these breakthroughs accessible to even people in the lower income bracket, we will become more accustomed to turn to scientists, doctors and technicians in moments of crisis and less to God. In this context, God loses as human progress forges ahead and gains as we remain ignorant and backward. Perhaps the most unbelievable realisation of all is to discover that, in this same context, God is more interested in losing than we are. For God wants us to turn to each other for aid whenever we can, to make use of our God-given talents and capacities, rather than to be ever asking him to help us with our home-work!

Lurking behind this simplistic "prayer-of-petitions-faith" is the implicit conviction that God should grant the prayers of all people, exactly as they specify or, at least, God should hear the prayers of some people – if not all "good people", then at least of all "true believers.[24] But a God who heard the prayers of all people as per their explicit instructions would be a God who wanted us all to remain stunted, spoilt children who would never grow up. If God were like that then all human endeavour for research, risk-filled discovery and enterprise, all courageous self-sacrificing love and adventure would lose all meaning! We'd all settle down to becoming like Tennyson's Lotos Eaters. And if God were to regularly listen to the prayers of his chosen few (on whatever count), then these molly-coddled prigs would be a spoilt brats we spoke of above and I am sure most of us would prefer the other alternative.

By all means should we make our prayers of petition to God in times of crisis, especially when a loved one is ill and languishing at death's door. It is

24 Who many of us identify with all those who belong to our own particular religion.

an act of faith in the fact that there is a power and a person who is stronger than the most incurable disease or for whom "nothing is impossible". Occasionally – only occasionally – God may work a miracle and heal someone, snatching him/her from death's door as a concrete sign that this conviction of ours is true, as an anticipatory sign of that day when all suffering and pain will be finally overcome and we all dwell together in God's loving embrace ... but this can't be done all the time, every time for everyone, or we'll be back in Lotosland once more. This is also why every miracle is, of course, primarily for the person who experiences (and his/her loved ones) but is also a message addressed to all the worlds "See, there is One who is stronger than any disease, stronger even than death! So, have confidence: death is not the end of life! It's just a change, a going into another room, as it were. It's not even the severing of a relationship. At death, only death dies, for it is really a passage to a fuller, lasting life." Meanwhile, God is always "at work" in us, whether we pray or not, giving us the courage and grace to resist evil, work for justice and wipe away tears, even those of a stranger!

"Religion is in the heart, not in the knees!" –Douglas William Jerrold

"I am just going to pray for you at St Paul's,
but with no very lively hope of success." –Sydney Smith

"Forgive, O Lord, my little jokes on Thee
And I'll forgive that great big one on me!" –Robert Frost

"If thou shouldst never see my face again,
Pray for my soul. More things are wrought by prayer
Than this world dreams of." –Alfred Lord Tennyson

Chapter 8

GOD AND EVIL

a. Introductory Notions

The agonising question as to how a world of so much suffering and pain could be reconciled with a God of love and power is one of such magnitude than many thinkers (especially those of a more mystical bent) suggest. Perhaps the best response we can cone tip with – and the only one worthy of a person of religious faith – would be a humble, trustful silence. But such an apparently hasty retreat behind the bulwark of "mystery" and blind faith can seem equally offensive to many of our contemporaries. Nor can we blame too easily those who scoff at such a responses a convenient escape that tries to cover up our ignorance, unfeelingness and laziness. It is also a safe bet to say that this phenomenon of evil and suffering is the biggest stumbling block to religious faith in the world and that every day more numbers are added to the list of lapsed believers and drop-outs from the ranks of those whose naive religious formation has not been able to help them integrate a painful human experience of suffering or the death of a loved one into a personal conviction concerning an all-powerful and all-loving God!

b. The Word "Theodicy"

The controversy has, indeed, spawned a specialised term to refer to the whole issue, theodicy. It comes from two Greek words, one of which, *theos*, is an old friend which means, as we all know, God; the other, *dike*, means justice. In other words, *theodicy* would be a word formed in parallel with jurisprudence and the law courts, where a defence lawyer would try to "justify" (prove innocent or "just") someone against whom some charge or the other had been introduced. In effect, the philosopher would see himself as the self-appointed defence lawyer for God, trying to acquit the all-loving and all-powerful divinity of the charge of the "colossal mismanagement of the cosmos". The whole endeavour smacks of the arrogant and the presumptuous (not to mention the blasphemous and the impious), in the sense that a puny human being has abrogated to himself the need to rush to the defence of the infinite whose behaviour, as seen by us from our limited human perspectives, has been found to be negligent! Be this as it may, it was the German rationalist Gottfried Leibnitz (1656-1716), who coined the phrase and preserved it in the title of a book ... whence it passed into the vocabulary of most major European languages!

But, however much we might ***regret*** the implications of the term, we cannot deny that it points, albeit clumsily, to a serious question that we can't afford to brush aside too easily. If we understandably baulk at "justifying" God, we certainly can try to understand God's "ways to man", as Milton put it. If there are proud and irreligious theodicies, there can also be humble and sensitive approaches to this mystery which we are struggling not to comprehend, but apprehend. This is all the more so when a fair-sized part of our effort consists in clearing up mistaken and misleading assumptions on which much of the issue is based. If we refuse to even wrestle, however unsuccessfully, with the "God and Evil" enigma, our faith might helplessly find itself mired in sinking sand in a moment of crisis'

c. A Problem? Or a Mystery?

Many thinkers prefer to speak of "the problem of evil" rather than dub it a "mystery". This is because they are averse to the penchant of religious leaders who try to squirm out of having to answer difficult questions by involving the useful cover-up of mystery! Thus, ignorance and lazy cowardice is given a respectable cloak of pseudo-religiosity: "It's all a mystery. Ours, not to question why, ours but to believe and die!

However, I would still persist in referring to the issue as a "mystery". But here I am not using it in the usual sense of "something too complicated for our limited minds to understand" and hence left aside as not meant for us to trouble ourselves about! Rather, I am using the term in the sense of Gabriel Marcel. I call evil a mystery in thesense that I do not see it as a baffling riddle, a disorder which I "view from the outside" (in other words, a typical "problem" in the Marcelian conception), but as a disturbing reality that has its roots within *me !* Evil is not a mere matter of "the wicked world out there" with its unjust structures, false values and criminal acts. There lurks within me a selfish craving, an urge to use others for my pleasure or benefit, a drive to exploit those weaker and poorer than myself the call of evil outside of me finds a responsive chord within me. It is a sobering and easily-forgotten truth that when we wrestle with the horrendous fact of evil and wickedness, we are struggling to make meaning: Out of a powerful aspect of ourselves. Indeed, a serious plumbing into the depths of our own self-seeking urge will more likely throw a lot more light on its nature and origin than a detached survey of it "from outside"!

d. Gathering Things, Old and New

Some of the points we have made earlier, especially in the last chapter, should have cleared up several of the misconceptions that further cloud a complex issue enough in this regard. For instance, we have noted that God does not make us die: death is something inevitably built into anything material: all material beings *must* perish or "fall apart" eventually! Again, we have tried to show that God does not – cannot – use a person "merely as a means"! Hence we have rejected most of those "naive theodicies" that seek to solve one problem by creating a far worse one in its place: God, we would be told, for instance, made such-and-such a road accident take place so that the victim might be an object lesson to others of the dangers of rash or drunken driving, or arranged for so-and-so to be born blind or mentally retarded in order to punish his/her parents for their misdeed or to teach them greater sensitivity or understanding. So we have some kind of "meaning' given to some people in their agony – but at the expense of others' suffering! Why should some people be so unimportant that their lives can be sacrificed for the good of others? Nor, as we have seen, does divine foreknowledge involve anything like divine predetermination! Thus, we have dispelled many doubts and difficulties about the mystery of evil, showing that they tire based on unfounded wrong assumptions.

But there still remain some questions to answer – and pretty radical ones at that. For instance, why is there within us a tendency to evil at all? Whence does it come? Could such a "natural tendency", involving a drive for selfishness, come originally from God? Why, indeed, did God make us free at all? Granted that he had the foreknowledge to see how we human would abuse this awesome potential? And what about all those other evils that can't he blamed on a perverse misuse of human freedom – cyclones, floods, earthquakes and so on? What about diseases like cancer and AIDS which all too often strike wholly innocent people, who've done nothing, to "bring on" the malady? What about little babies being born deformed or handicapped? Was it really necessary for God to have given us a world in which there would be killer viruses and microbes that could cause lingering, painful deaths? Finally, why did God make us "embodied"? After all, it is only because we have bodies that we can feel pain, sicken, grow old and eventually die. All this would have been avoided if God had created us bodiless spirits, like angels. Then we would be immune to suffering, decease and death. We must grapple with each of these questions in turn, upsetting though they be.

e. Reviewing God's Omnipotence

God, is omnipotent, or almighty, to use a more Anglo-Saxon word. But, all too often, people think that this means that God can do "anything at all," including drawing square circles, making a whole which is smaller than a part and even (as some people think is the case in the Christian doctrine of the Trinity) where 3 = 1! But this is definitely not the case!

God cannot do anything that involves a flat contradiction. To do that God would have to contradict his/her own nature which is also Truth. God cannot make square circles and all that sort of thing, just as God cannot sin. The fact that God cannot do these things, as we shall see, does not stem from some lack within God, but from something self-destructive in the thing, itself.

Now, the fact that I can sin and God can't, might make it seem, at first sight that I am freer than God – I am able to do something God cannot bring Himself/Herself to do! A little reflection should help us to realise that the ability to sin is not so much an expression of freedom as resulting from a deficiency of freedom! Freedom, remember, is a means to an end: Liberation! Because we are not fully actualised or liberated, it is possible for us to choose something which brings us fulfillment in only one isolated area of our many-faceted existence, while ending up in harming our total personal growth (in other words, such an act makes us less liberated).

We will try to show, quite soon, that God *cannot* make finite persons who are not embodied, not placed in an evolutionary world (a world where things are not finished products) and so on. For God to do this would be equivalent to making square circles or round triangles. If God *could* have done otherwise but did not, then one can raise valid doubts about God's goodness or omnipotence. But such was not the case, as I hope to show as we proceed.

f. Approaches to the Issue

The way one views a problem cannot but have an impact on the kind of response one would make to it. The man who views something as a mere stumbling block will react to it in a very different way from the one who sees it as a stepping stone! A river may be viewed plainly and simply as a nuisance, something to be "got over" as quickly as possible so as to get on with one's proper goal and purpose. Or one can see it as a welcome break from the ardours of the quest, dive in; relish the river, enjoy a swim and then, with renewed and rejuvenated spirit, re-commit oneself to what lies ahead.

So it is with the mystery of evil. Of course, I am not trying to advocate as some theodicies do that "there is nothing either good or bad but thinking makes it so" (Shakespeare's *Hamlet* II, 2). Try telling an Indian Dalit whose wife has been raped, stripped naked and paraded in the market place that what happened to that poor woman was not "evil in itself." Or try to uphold such a view if you were a person wasting away with AIDS or cancer! And does one really agree that the only difference, between a terrorist who sets off a time-bomb in a crowded marketplace and a social worker who takes the mangled victims of the blast and the orphaned children of those who died there by is the perspective from which we view them? What I" mean is saying that the agonies of a cancer person will summon forth different practical responses from one who views them as a punishment for the person's sin, or those of his parents or those committed in a former life or by one who views them as not directly willed by God at all! Similarly, evil looked at against a static understanding of reality will be made sense of – and responded to – in a totally different way from evil considered within a dynamic world-view.

At first sight, it would appear that the world around us affords us nothing but a sorry spectacle of things gone awry. And which of us has not, at some time or the other felt stirred (and perhaps still feels stirred?) to "get up and do something about the mess the world is in"? Like Hamlet of old, we recognise that "something is rotten in the state of Denmark", or India, or wherever the world over. But soon our youthful enthusiasm and idealism baulks as we begin to realise the immensity of the task we are trying to take on. Once again, with *Hamlet*,[25] we tend to cry out, in effect:

> The time is out of joint. O, cursed spite,
> That ever I was born to set it right!

And most of us, sooner or later, give up in disgust. The task is too enormous, we tell ourselves. We put our earlier idealism aside. "It's just a romantic phase we all have to go through as youths!" we tell ourselves. And the majority of us resign ourselves sadly (and cynically) to the status quo. "Nothing can be done about it, really!" we say as if to excuse our opting out.

g. Two Sources

As for "the mess the world is in", well, these seem to stem from two clearly defined and separate causes. One is the result of deliberate human choice. This would include the ill treatment of Dalits in India, the various internecine tribal conflicts that bedevil Africa from time to time, the tragedies of Chechnya and the Kosovo, to mention a few. All these are obviously the consequence of deliberate human choice. Human beings – for whatever justifiable or non-justifiable reasons – wilfully decided to make these awful events – come to pass. But there is a whole series of other unpleasant things which no human being wished for or caused, at least, not consciously and deliberately. These include the terrible floods that recently wrought havoc in Kerala and Maharashtra, the ghastly and mysterious illness that ruthlessly carries of a young teenager in the

25 I.5.190-191.

bloom of promise, the deformed little baby born to horrified parents. Nobody wanted these things to happen: just the contrary!

We could also speak of a third category of painful event, certainly due to human causality, but not deliberately intended. This is the whole area of human error or "accident". Thus, due to a pilot's carelessness, a plane crashes and he and passengers are killed. A cricket player hits the ball and it zooms to the boundary ... where it strikes a spectator on the temple and he dies! An enquiry might or might not exonerate the pilot from "culpable error" in the first place or not; what is certain is that he didn't consciously choose, with grim efficiency to take his own life and that of his passengers! In other words, though this tragedy was due to human instrumentality (our "first source" above), it cannot be put down as an "abuse of human freedom", but rather as an unfortunate consequence of human frailty and infirmity.

h. "Nature, Red in Tooth and Claw!"

However, much environmentalists may romanticise and glorify Nature and "man in the pure state of Nature" as a "noble savage", the fact remains that Nature is *not* founded on non-violent principles (as per Gandhiji). As Tennyson put it in his *In Memoriam*,[26] "Nature (is) red in tooth and claw!" If one accepts Evolution (and there seem to be more data in favour of it than against it), then we have to admit that "survival of the fittest" and "might is right" have been the bloody and brutal laws that separated the survivors from the losers. One could, of course, point out that it was not sheer physical strength and brawn that decided things, for, on that count alone, humans would never have been able to prevail. Whatever wiped out those huge carnivorous saurians of prehistoric times (the fall of a timely series of meteors?), puny man had still to contend with wooly mammoths, mastodons and sabre-toothed tigers – all more than a match for his puny capabilities. We survived because our emergent intellect (and our having learned to walk upright on two feet) made us superior to all those powerful beasts, which we were able to kill and devour before they could render us the same service!

But, even today, in the sea the bigger fish prey upon the smaller fish and on land the bigger denizens hunt and kill the smaller ones for dinner. At every turn, and twist we masscare millions of mocrobes. By virtue of a grim kind of poetic justice, *en revenge,* a tiny germ or virus can snuff out the life of an organism vastly greater than itself. Then there is the phenomenon of the colossal waste that governs the laws of nature. Of the billions of spermatazoa and ova that come into being, only a miniscule fraction go on to constitute a single foetus: the rest are cast aside and forgotten. Indeed lower animals spawn their offspring in prolific abundance because only a tiny proportion has

26 lvi.

any hope of growing into adulthood, And there seems to be a curious logic (to say the least) in the fact that a huge animal, like an elephant is a vegetarian and is quite satisfied with a diet of leaves whereas a tiny cat feels the need to terrorise, hurt and kill a mouse in order to fulfil its appetite! Details such as these militate against over-hasty, simplistic and glib paeans of praise in honour of the "natural order" and naive justifications of God's marvellous ways!

i. Augustine vs Irenaeus

I am indeed grateful to the British scholar, John Hick, who in his epochal work, *Evil and the God of Love*,[27] drew my attention to the fact that there have been basically two approaches to the theodicy in the Western tradition: one is better known, more generally followed and received more conscious thematic elaboration – that of St Augustine of Hippo (354–430). The other dates from much earlier, is less known and did not receive any studied formulation and was not so extensively passed on developed by St Ireaneus of Lyons (140-202). Whether one is Christian or not, whether one agrees with their interpretation of *Genesis* or not, what they have to say is worth listening to. Augustanl's approach was based on a more static, pessimistic view of the human person and of the world and came to be generally upheld by the Roman tradition in Christianity which, for political and other reasons, became the dominant one. Irenaeus1 view Implied a more optimistic perspective and was developed from a more dynamic vision of reality and became characteristic of the Greek school of Christianity. Irenaeus was not a systematic thinker like Augustine and it was the Augustinian-Roman way of looking at things that won the day over the Greek alternative and, in spite of the contribution of St Clement of Alexandria (150-214), the Irenean-Greek theory never really got the chance to work itself out into the teachings of a well-established school. Nevertheless, from time to time, various thinkers – both Christian and non-Christian – came up with clumsy and more thought out ideas that could have gained more precision and depth had they known of, or drawn upon, the Irenean insight! I myself had been an "uneasy Christian" as far as Augustinian theodicy was concerned. I had worked out my own tentative response, nurtured by my readings of various Holy Books and my own theological studies (which came, as far as I am concerned, rather late in my life). I struggled to express my ideas in a stumbling, hesitant form that led certain champions of orthodoxy to opine that I had abandoned all belief in petitionary prayer and divine providence … if not in the Christian conception of God, altogether! It was an immense relief for me to have come across Hick relatively slim but scholarly and deep study in the early 80s, just after my return from studies abroad. How delighted I was to find that my awkward forays into personal theologising (which smacked to

27 Glasgow, Collins, 1978 (reprint).

heresy to many of my companions) could, with a bit more critical reflection, be worked into a solid doctrine, inspired by the research of a contemporary committed Christian (though non-Catholic) thinker. And it was a further "shot in the arm" to discover that such a view could find root in another saint of the Church, whose views pre-dated Augustine's and even went back to the earliest beginnings of Christian thought.

Finally, I would like to stress the point, once again, that in this section I am going to speak only of Irenaeus and Augustine's implicit *philosophy*: I am not discussing their explicit theology, which would be very interesting and insightful, perhaps, for Christians in search of a more dynamic and liberative (while quite orthodox) understanding of their faith. I am indeed grateful to John Hick for sharping the fruits of his pioneering research with me. Indeed, I find them particularly relevant to the Indian scene!

j. Where Their Views Differ

Perhaps we should let John Hick summarise for us the key elements whereby the dynamic understanding of the Adam and Eve story of Iraneous differ from the static conception of Augustin. After all, it was Hick that pioneered this breakthrough discovery in his research:

> Instead of the [Augustinian] doctrine that man has created finitely perfect and then incomprehensibly destroyed his own perfection and plunged into sin and misery, Irenaeue suggests that man was created as an immature, imperfect creature who was to undergo moral development and growth and finally be brought to the perfection intended for him by his maker. Instead of the fall of Adam being presented, as in the Augustinain tradition, as an utterly malignant and catastrophic event, completely disrupting God's plan, Irenaeus pictured it as something that occurred in the childhood of the race, an understandable lapse due to weakness and immaturity rather than an adult crime full of malice and pregnant with perpetual guilt. And, Instead of the Augustinian view of life's trials are a divine punishment for Adam's sin, Irenaeus sees our world of mingled good and evil as a divinely appointed environment for man's development towards the perfection that represents the fulfillment of God's purpose for him.

k. Implications of Augustinian View

What concerns us here is the difference in Implication of these two rival interpretations of the Genesis myth. It is the respective philosophy of the human person and our environment that is relevant for us in elaborating a new theodicy, one which is more in keeping with the present-day dynamic vision of reality that we share, rather than the out-dated static perspective of the traditional one.

In Augustine's understanding, Adam and Eve were created by God as perfect am finite beings could be. They could not have been absolutely perfect, of course, because that would have required them to be uncreated and Infinite (which is clearly impossible!). But he saw them as endowed with "preternatural gifts," such as immortality and the fullness of knowledge. As a result of the "Fall", whereby Adam and Eve failed the "test" God had given them, the couple forfeited ("fell from grace") the high estate God had favoured them with, far above and beyond their natural deserts and exigencies. Their nature became corrupt, "wounded" and prey to the various evil tendencies and other pathways to sin that they had open themselves to by their wicked act. Catholics and Protestants might differ as to precisely the degree of corruption that entered human life and how much of freewill survived the onslaught, but all seemed to agree that "concupiscence"' (understood as the inner prompting to evil consequent upon the "original sin" of Adam and Eve) had begun to vitiate all our best efforts. This is how, in the Augustinian perspective, we are to account for the tendency to evil we notice in ourselves.

Furthermore, not only has our very nature become "wounded" incurably by "original sin", our whole life had to be lived out in punishment in this world which was meant to be a "vale of tears". No longer had we access to the pleasant Garden of Eden which was God's original plan for us, if only Adam and Eve had exercised a little more self-control!

It should be noticed, just for the record, that there is nothing in the Genesis story to corroborate the notion that our "first parents" enjoyed any "supernatural" qualities, as St Augustine was so convinced about. In other words, the original myth doesn't imply that there was "a Fall", since there was no previously elevated state to fall from! Nor is there any use of the term "original sin" anywhere in the Bible! It simply records the gradual universalisation of sin, as humankind freely and progressively turned its collective back on God's love and God's call. Today, most theologians and biblical scholars would prefer to speak of "cosmic" or "universal" sin and recognise that the Adamic myth is interested in throwing light upon the nature of sin and its consequences (alienation from "fellow humans and from nature"): it is not interested in telling us how sin began, what was the first historical sin committed and such like matters.

l. Augustine in His Own Words

In his celebrated *City of God*,[28] as in other writings, Augustine presents us with a detailed description of the ideal condition of Adam and Eve in Paradise, prior to their fatal "Fall". They were endowed with Immortality (they would

28 Augustine, St and Marcus Dods. *The City of God*. Lexington, KY: Amazon Create Space, 2018.

never die, nor would they grow old), they had total control over their bodily passions and rejoiced in infallible moral judgments and other insights. They lived in close intimacy with God and their love for God was *imperturbatus* (undisturbed, unclouded, untroubled). They experienced no "inner tendency to evil" in them originally, no hankering for the forbidden fruit. In Augustine's own words,

> In Paradise, then, man ... lived in the enjoyment of God, and was good by God's goodness; he lived without any want, and had it in his power to live eternally. He had food that he might not hunger, drink that he might not thirst, the tree of life that old age might wither him. There was in his body, no corruption, nor seed of corruption, which could produce in him any pleasant sensation. He feared no inward desires, no outward accident. Soundest health blessed his body, absolute tranquillity his soul. As in Paradise there was no excessive heat nor cold, so its inhabitants were exempt from the vicissitudes of fear and desire. No sadness of any kind was there, nor any foolish joy; true gladness ceaselessly flowed from the presence of God, who was loved 'out of a pure heart and a good conscience and faith unfeigned.' The honest love of husband and wife made a sure harmony between them. Body and spirit worked harmoniously together, and the commitment was kept without labour. No languor made their leisure wearisome; no sleepiness interrupted their desire to labour.

In all this, Augustine was but following some ancient rabbinical traditions, which also idealised Adam's state, envisioning him as endowed with extraordinary stature, dazzling physical beauty, all-surpassing wisdom and so on, as Hick has noted.

m. The Difficulty with Augustine's Approach

Now, the main reason why Augustine "piled it on", making Adam and Eve as perfect creatures as possible and situating them in an idyllic utopia, was because he was overeager to get God "off the hook" for having created anything that was evil – not even indirectly, remotely or even potentially. This zeal did more credit to his heart than to his head for, in his determination to solve one problem, he created another, far more disastrous in its implications than the first one, as far as we humans are concerned. For, if Augustine succeeded to establish, in one deft description, the innocence of God and the abhorrent perversity of the human person in bringing sin (and its consequent punishments) into this world, he presents us, by the same count, with the absurdity of a finite creature creating evil *ex nihilo*, out of nothing-ness. As Hick asks, "How, then, we may well wonder, did sin enter into this paradisal state?" "How is it that Adam and Eve, with all their perfect maturity and intelligence, their lack of "inner concupiscence" and perfect self-control, were unable to resist the blandishments of a talking snake? Augustine, not very logically, recognised that since "our first parents" were able to succumb to the temptations of the devil there had to be some kind of "evil will" in them: "the wicked desire already existed in them and the open sin was but its consequence." As for this evil desire it was nothing other than the will to be self-sufficient. Thus we have a "theodicy" which, in order to establish God's innocence of all evil, depicts God as having created humans with created freedom and who thereby couldn't but sin and then, because of this would load punishment after punishment, not only on them, but also on all their offspring ever after, for these were already "seminally present" in Adam's loins and were, therefore, somehow guilty along with him. It would be better to pass over those passages where the great "Doctor of the Church" finds himself hurled along, by the very force of his arguments, into saying that – in effect – God created some people with the express purpose of saving them and others (the vast majority, by far) with the express purposes of damning them. Indeed, a strange theodicy, that ends up making God a petty, revengeful tyrant!

n. Augustine's Understanding of Evil/Sin

The traditional Augustinian understanding of evil, which Aquinas and the entire Western Christian tradition as a whole (with rare exceptions) follows sees evil as *privatio boni*, a privation of good, that is, a lack of some positive quality that was supposed to be there. Evil, as such, doesn't really exist. It is not. Metaphysically speaking, evil is not a positive entity but, as Aquinas would put it, a "relative non-being". Evil is not so much a being as the absence of a being, to be more precise, it is the absence of something positive in some reality. The Inability to see in a human being is an evil, because humans are supposed to see. But the inability of, say, a table or a stone, to see is not an evil for neither of these beings are meant to see. Nor is a human's inability to soar through the sky like an eagle or to live in water like a salmon an evil, for humans are not supposed to have the qualities that would enable them to do these things. Were an eagle or a salmon to lack these abilities, respectively, they would be "evils" for them, however. Yet, for Leibnitz (the German rationalist of the eighteenth century), *anv* lack, whether due or not, is an evil, a "metaphysical evil", as he would say. Thus, the fact that we "lack" some of God's qualities – infiniteness, omniscience (all-knowingness), omnipotence (all-powerfulness), etc. – would be examples of "metaphysical evil" for him. So, would the dog's inability to speak, a salmon's inability to fly and an eagle's inability to plunge underwater! I don't see it very meaningful to refer to the lack of something which wasn't supposed to be there in the first place, as an "evil" by any name whatsoever!

Following upon his general definition of evil (which I have outlined above), Augustine proceeds to sub-divide it into two broad categories, physical evil and moral evil. Physical evil is the absence of some due physical quality in a material being. All the examples given above, of blindness in humans or an eagle's inability to fly could be cited here. Moral evil is defined as the absence of a due orientation in a free personal act. Thus, a lie is a moral evil, because it implies the absence of a due orientation in an act of speech. The natural purpose of speech (its "due orientation") is to communicate, to share one's knowledge and a lie does just the opposite.

Now Augustine's definition is very convenient – for God! Inasmuch as it defines evil as a relative non-being, as a non-being *in itself*, it requires no "maker". So, God can't be "blamed" for its existence – since it has no existence, strictly speaking – it is the mere absence of existence in something. This is very ingenuous, but it hardly holds water in the light of modern developments in the medical sciences. For the "physical evil" of sickness is much more than the mere "absence of health". We know that cancer, leprosy and AIDS are caused by the actual presence of something in the devastated body that is causing these deadly-diseases. Besides if each and every malady – from a tooth-ache to kidney failure – were a mere "absence of health" how would we distinguish one illness from another? Assuredly it's the *presence* of some – awfully real in-one person that gives him a head-ache as opposed to someone else's measles!

o. Irenaeus' Understanding of Evil

Let us, once again, recall that Irenaeus, unlike Augustine, was not a systematic thinker and didn't put down his ideas in an orderly manner in well thought out treatises (which is one of the reasons why his views were not so well known as Augustine's). We have to seek for and cull his views from scattered asides here and there in various writings and notes which he jotted down as occasion and polemic demanded. Especially relevant in this regard is a text which was entitled (probably by someone other than Irenaeus himself), rather unecumenically, *Against the Heretics*.[29] His understanding of evil must be extracted from the context of his dynamic (we might prefer to say, evolutionary) understanding of creation, especially of the human person. Evil is a kind of unfinishedness, a stage of as yet unrealised development in the evolutionary process. It sometimes results from the clash of different process of development colliding with each other. The need of the lion to grow clashes with the need of the deer to grow and the "natural development" of the former results in the "physical evil" of the hurt and death of the latter. So, too, the "natural development" of the virus or microbe to grow ends up in its entering a living organism and bringing about sickness, and perhaps death, in a plant, an animal or a human. Adam and Eve's sin was seen by Irenaeus as moral evil all right, but as a kind of inevitable possibility in the context of their immaturity

29 Irenaeus, St Bp of Lyons, *Five Books of S. Irenaeus: Bishop of Lyons, against Heresies*. Oxford: J. Parker, 1872.

as they struggled within their environment to attain the goal of responsible and mature freedom as adults. Moral evil is an inevitable option to humans in their finiteness as they make their stumbling way to becoming fully-human, fully alive (another catch-phrase from Irenaeus). This doesn't mean that humans can't be blamed for their wrong choices. Of course we are guilty of all the rapes and murders – or even petty lies and unfaithfulnesses – of which we are responsible. How blameworthy we are depends on how knowledgable and "free" we were at the time of doing these acts, but they must be all put in their proper context. If no one is perfectly mature and fully in command of his/her situation, no one who's not mentally deficient or an addict can be "let off" his or her peccadilloes and well-planned crimes! As for "physical evils" these are not seen (as Augustine did) as divine punishments let loose upon hapless humans. Rather, they are the unavoidable necessary consequences attendant on that evolutionary world which alone would give us finite persons the required environment for growing into mature and responsible adults. As for human error, accidents and mistakes that sometimes lead to suffering, pain and death, these are the natural result of our inherent frailty as embodied beings. This, in a nutshell is the Ireanean-based theodicy which we shall uphold. Now let us go into it in more detail.

p. "Epistemic Distance"

"Epistemic" comes from *episteme* (a Greek word), and means "having to do with knowledge (*Epistemology* is the official name for "the philosophy of knowledge" It is to John Hick that I am indebted for this key term in my theodicy. When God creates a finite person, God must do so in such a way that he/ she be given a certain "distance" to traverse in order to grow to the fullness of maturity. Obviously, this can't be a physical distance to cross over and "epistemic", would seem to be the best term.

An adult person worthy of the name is one who is able to make free and responsible decisions and, thereby, be able to love in as selfless and unconditional way as is humanly possible. None of us is ever "perfectly human", capable of absolutely mature, responsible and unconditional decision-making and loving: that is a kind of goal that we're forever approaching and falling away from. Thus, authentic personhood is not something we can be "given on a plate", as it were-; rather, is it something that we must strive towards, fighting against our passions, our immaturities and our self-love. We must struggle towards, self-awareness, gradually getting to distinguish our real true selves, from the "false consciousness" that psychologists, have spoken of , those layers of wrong ideas and false notions: of superiority (based on gender, ethnic origin, colour of skin and so on that questionable social conditioning has foisted upon us). All too many of us are so uncritical of ourselves and our social roots that we tend to "blindly follow the crowd" and, consequently, our "free" actions are more the brain-washed responses of a thoroughly conditioned individual who is reacting, rather than acting, in response to the situations around us. If God wants finite persons to exist, God has no other choice than to bring us into existence in such a way that we have to attain personhood as the fruit of our efforts, trials and failures, relentlessly pursuing that as an elusive goal. In a very real sense, persons aren't born, but made and it is the persons themselves who have to do the making! We see this happening all around us and we are not through the process as far as each of us is concerned. Infants grow through babyhood, gradually learning to became aware of others and their needs and slowly, as they stumble through the awkwardness of adolescence, learning to be more other-centred as they form their first full-blooded friendships and "boy-girl relationships". What helps us most in this long process is having experienced true love in our families – having experienced the love of our parents for us, for each other and for our brothers and sisters and vice versa. When these are glaringly absent, it becomes more' difficult – but not impossible – to grow in mature love and freedom. Many people help us, our teachers, companions, friends, religious personages ... but these can also figure as hindrances to us in the great adventure of' "growing up", which is what "epistemic distance" is all about. This is very evidently an insight which is rooted in a dynamic, evolutionary understanding of reality in general, and of the human person in particular.

q. Embodiedness: A Pre-Condition for Epistemic Distance

A finite, created person *must* be embodied. Embodiedness provides us the ideal (and the only!) context wherein we can struggle and persevere in relentless effort towards authentic personhood. Knowledge doesn't come easy to an embodied being, as we know – neither knowledge of the external world, nor knowledge of ourselves.. We all know how true it is that "genius is 1% inspiration and 99% perspiration". We study, we research, we inch our way to finding remedies for "incurable" diseases, for "insoluble" problems. We build upon the mistakes and breakthroughs of others. Pioneers dare to dream and ask, "Why not?", braving the scorn, the rejection and neglect of academically mediocre people in power who want to retain their strangle-hold of how people think about human limitations, they starve, lonely in their garrets and make-shift workplaces. Sometimes their sacrifices are eventually crowned with success. Often, they are not. But they persevere. They remain true to their convictions. If they do not reach their goals themselves, they make it a little easier for the next dreamer, the next adventurer, the next intrepid explorer who comes after... And thus, not only do they grow in humanness through their own efforts, they hand on the baton to the next generation, inspiring and motivating others to aim for such higher, nobler goals.

So, too, does each of us battle on as we seek to understand our deeper truer selves. We seek enlightenment, self-realisation, self-awareness. We ask our companions how we "come across" to them. "Who am I, really?" we ask ourselves. "Why am I here? What can I do to make of my life something meaningful and worthwhile?" We, every once in a while, become complacent. We think we "have arrived" have finally "come of age", have got "everything under control". Then along comes an unexpected encounter, we are swept off our feet and end up saying and doing things that make us blush. Our "shadow side" suddenly emerges and throw into disarray all our well-disciplined lives, our finest friendships and loves. We are humiliated. We ask for forgiveness. We try again. We don't give up. Sometimes we are helped along the way by the understanding smile or encouraging word from a person who cares. Sometimes we have to manage by ourselves as best we can. We resume the demanding, challenging journey to personhood, to mature loving, to responsible freedom!

Embodiedness, with its consequent context of struggling to self-awareness, self-mastery and self-realisation, its renewed commitment to know, to understand ourselves, all around us, embodiedness provides us with that unique, irreplaceable situation through which we can make this journey to maturity, to authenticity. Our enfleshment, far from being something to regret, is the necessary condition for us to attain full personhood. We are not discarnate spirits; we are incarnate, enfleshed spirits and this is the only way created spirits can ever attain personhood. Our ups and down, our hurts failures, our sorrows and joys aren't just "punishments" or "rewards" allotted us by God in response to our sinful or virtuous acts, or as part of the punishment left over for the fault of our "first parents"! They are the very means whereby we become those truly free and loving persons we are called to be and which, by every fibre of our being, we yearn to be. What else could provide us with this "epistemic distance" if it were not our embodiedness?

r. An Evolving World, Another Pre-Condition for Epistemic Distance

The above should make it abundantly clear that this epistemic distance has to be traversed by free beings and no other. For how could we learn to love through making sacrifices, taking risks and persevering in the face of failure and setback if we were not capable of free choice and personal resolve? Nor am I requiring us to have a kind of sovereign, inviolate and inhuman freedom, in solitary isolation from our situation, as Jean-Paul Sartre, the French existentialist envisages. Ours is an incarnate human freedom rooted in, and in response to, our world. This is its grandeur, as Paul Ricoeur would recognise. It's a freedom that cannot be given us "on a plate"; it is a freedom that has to be fought for, struggling against enslaving passions and societal brainwashing, overcoming complex lurking pressures, internal and external. Now, such a freedom can only be built up in an evolutionary world. It cannot be attained in a nice "finished product world" – as David Hume wants God to have provided us with. In such a set-up, ideal for pampered pets, not for "persons-in-the-making", everything would be ordered around our convenience." The temperature would be just right, meals would arrive at the right time and properly cooked, we'd be given just the right amount of exercise not to let us get too fat and sloppy. But an environment that would mediate the epistemic distance in question would have to be that of an evolutionary world, one where we'd have apt opportunity for struggle, research and quest, as I've described just above. Such a world would be a "non-finished-product" world, a dynamic one that is yet "in the making". Hence arises the possibility of earthquakes, cyclones and suddenly active volcanoes – all part of the evolutionary packaged deal. Only in such a demanding and challenging set-up will we find occasion to exercise, our resourcefulness, initiative and daring. Were parents to surround their beloved children with a kind of *cordon sanitaire* of protective servants, eager to prevent them from every mishap or hurt and catering to their each and every whim as soon as it was manifest ... their offspring would remain perpetually stunted children. Such a world would soon become boring: there would be no scope for adventure and excitement, no opportunity for courage and daring, little challenge to mature love and friendship. Nor has God abandoned us, with typical deistic unconcern, to a hostile world. We have intelligence, freedom and talents which must be developed, built up through the shared successes and failure of our fellows. God's grace and inspiration is there, available to us in and through personal exchanges in the depths of each individual, but also through the events of everyday life as well as the various religious traditions, as I have already mentioned. And even if we "lose" and our lives are cut short by some tragic event or the goals we dreamt off are not realised by us, still all is not lost. The grave is not the end!

s. Whence Comes Our Self-Seeking Urge?

We all recognise within us a selfish, domineering and grasping urge which, ever so often, contradicts and even overturns our most idealistic and altruistic ideals. Something within us seems to respond to "the call of the wild" from outside and we end up bullying the weak, exploiting the poor and taking advantage of the helpless. Whence comes this ingrained "law of the Jungle" in us, this "might is right" and "survival of the fittest" drive within us? Is it nothing but the "wounding" we have done to ourselves and our freedom by "participating" in original sin through having somehow been "in the loins of Adam" when he committed his terrible crime, as Augustine would have it. I think not. Once again, it's got to do with evolution. 'In the dim and distant eons ago of pre-historic times, these were the very laws that helped us to overcome gigantic rivals who out classed us in size and strength. Our courageous ape-like ancestors, with the passage of time, interiorised as instinctive and reflex strategies, these principles in the daily confrontation of hulking carnivorous monsters with our derisory size and puny strength. As mentioned earlier, it was our having learnt to stand upright and develop our mental powers that won us our hard-earned victory. These defence mechanisms and "guidelines for the fray" have lingered on and that is how we find them suddenly emerge to channel our careless reactions, from time to time. Now that the horrendous jungle world of the Cromagnon and the Neanderthal is no longer with us, we must set about controlling these urges and drives which once had their positive and necessary role to play in our development and evolutionary ascent. Some of us have acquired, through conscious effort, more control of our id and libido than others. On the whole, considerable progress *has* been made. All in all, our world has become more "civilised", more "refined": human life is no longer "nasty, brutish and short", with "man behaving unto man as a beast" as Thomas Hobbes (1588-1679) once described those remote and awful times. We don't meet roving bands of "robber- barons" *arid* "bandit-chiefs" raping and pillaging the countryside all about us. Governments are rejecting torture and inhuman penalties for minor and major crimes. Even capital punishment is coming under fire. There is a mushrooming of protest groups against cruelty to animals, police brutality, the consumer society. People are coming together to protect endangered species, women, gays and oppressed people all over the earth. And it is not just "young people" who are doing all this. Many of us want to go deeper into self-awareness, self-mastery and self-control. Men, women and even children are signing up for courses on yoga, transcendental meditation, Buddhist retreats. Others seek to "sublimate" these "violent urges" in a more healthy, socially helpful manner, through sports, adventure and various demanding outdoor activities. We're also beginning to realise that, rather than seeking to suppress or deny our "shadow side", we'd do better to find more constructive ways to let it express itself. Overcoming, or rather re-orienting our "self-seeking and violent urge" is part of the agenda in traversing epistemic distance. God helps us in this area, too.

t. What about Handicapped Babies?

From what we have said above, it should be clear that we cannot countenance those who try to "explain away" the plight of new-born babies who are physically or mentally impaired by saying that this is either due to some punishment being visited on the parents (usually ascribed to "pre-marital sex"!) or, on a somewhat more "charitable" note, saying that God was teaching the couple, thereby, to grow in unconditional love or some other human quality. All these deplorable "explanations" imply that God is treating the innocent little one as merely a means. Such an act goes against all fundamental human rights and dignity and is totally abhorrent to all that God is!

Many such children are born in slums, favellas and in conditions of misery and acute deprivation. In such cases, the suffering of the affected little one's is due to the malnourished mother not having had access to proper food and medical guidance. Very often, even in advanced stages of her pregnancy, she has to perform protracted hours of demanding work, including fetch water from rather long distances. Is it any wonder that she gives birth to an infant with severe vitamin deficiencies, from which result all kinds of debilities and deficiencies? Of course, occasionally, such infants are born of mothers in fairly well-to-do families, who have the best of medicare and a proper diet. In some cases, the plight of the child can be put down to sheer negligence or carelessness on the part of the mother: her consumption of alarming amount of alcohol, indulging in narcotic substances or chain-smoking. At times, it is nobody's "fault": the mother unwittingly passes on to the child some genetic defect or there is some "incompatibility problem" between the parents' blood. On rare occasions, some of the drugs and other medicaments given to the nursing, mother can have harmful side-effects on the child. The development of medical science and research has made great strides in remedying, if not avoiding, many of these malfunctionings.

u. Conclusion

Every aspect of the sorry spectacle of human suffering and evil takes on a wholly new mince when viewed against the backdrop of a more dynamic, 'evolutionary world, such as the one worked out', however sketchily by Irenaeus. Fleshing out the skeleton in the light of modern development and research, while introducing the key insightful notion of John Hick, "epistemic distance", have stood us in good stead as we "wrestled with the angel", as it were, trying to make sense of the enigmatic mystery as to why bad things happen to good people – or *vice versa*! Such disturbing phenomena clamour for an answer. Well, we have ventured a response. I do not claim that it is a perfect one, dispelling all possible, further scope for doubt and completely explaining away the mystery (as if one could ever hope to do that). But I do claim that this is a more meaningful "theodicy" than the traditional alternative provided us by Augustine.

Taking a more dynamic (rather than the old static) conception of the world as our base is not just to be more "trendy" or "mod"; it is also something "that strikes a responsive chord in many a heart. It's more challenging to see evil, not so much as a mere "lack" of something somewhere, but as an as yet unrealised stage of fulfillment in a growth process. An evolutionary world, the necessary context of "person-making" motivates us to action for justice; seeing the world as a place of punishment, a "vale of tears" where, from time to time, we must be put to torture, only teaches us to be passive, resigned and submissive. It is more wholesome to see our bodies as positive means of access to authentic human personhood and responsible freedom, rather than despicable wounded aspects of our tainted human nature. There still remain "areas of darkness", bits and pieces of "unanswered questions" (or unsatisfactorily answered questions), but I have derived enough vision and insight from this dynamic approach to be able to carry these peacefully to my grave.

There remains, however, one question which I have ignored so far: what about angels? Many religions, including Judaism, Christianity and-Islam, have a place for these beings, usually depicted as winged, white-robed and handsome young men, in their mythology. If we grant that embodiedness is necessary to provide the proper epistemic distance for personal self-realisation, we must write off all angels as symbolic elements in the theologisations of these faith, but not corresponding to anything in reality and truth. This I have no qualms about doing, though many may feel that this is "one fell swoop" too many. In which case, they would have to return to the Augustianian perspective or try to find some way of integrating angels into an evolutionary world view.

"Happiness is beneficial for the body, but it is grief that develops the powers of the mind." –Marcel Proust

"It is such a secret place, the land of tears!" –Antoine de St. Exupery

"A man who fears suffering is already suffering from what he fears." –Michel de Montaigne

Appendix to Chapter 8

THE HINDU DOCTRINE OF REBIRTH

a. Introductory Ideas

The Hindu doctrine that, when we die, we will return (to be more precise, our souls will return) to earth, animating another body – sometimes human, sometimes sub-human – is, among other things, also a "theodicy". It seeks to explain why some people are born into misery and other into prosperity, 'why bad things happen to apparently good people (and *vice versa*) Hence I am including a critical reflection on this extremely interesting notion, which is believed by over 800,000,000 million people in India and has, for centuries inspired many to live ethically upright and committed lives.

b. Widespread Roots

Some kind of belief that, when we die, our souls are "reborn" into other bodies is found in many ancient cultures. In such a conception, of course, personal identity is one with the soul. I am a soul, I *have* a body: my body is seen as something external to me, an appendage. I can assume or discard at will, like a piece of clothing. This has also been called *metempsychosis* or *palingenesis* (Greek versions of the same name). In India, Hindus, Buddhists and Jains still believe in it and it has won many adherents in Europe and USA, too. Traces of such a belief can be found even nowadays, among such disparate traditions and cultures as that of the Ibp tribe in South East Nigeria, as well as the natives of the New Guinea coast. In the West", Plato[30] ranks as one of its most illustrious proponents. The *Rg-Veda*. the most ancient of all India's sacred texts, makes no mention of it, though the notion is clearly enshrined in later Vedantic and Buddhist texts. It figures prominently in the *Gita*:

---

30 cf *Timaus*.

> Just as the soul in this body passes through Childhood, youth and old age.
> So too (at death) it passes into another bodv.
> A wise man is not perplexed by that. (II, 13)
> As a man casts off worn-out garments And takes other that are new,
> So does the embodied soul cast off
> Its worn-out bodies and enter into others that are-new. (II, 22)
> For death is certain for the born,
> And re-birth is certain for the dead;
> Therefore you should not grieve For what is inevitable. (II, 27)

c. The Doctrine

The three great religions of India, however much they may differ among themselves, share a common set of views concerning the after-life. These may be summed up as follows:

- A theory of rebirth that postulates a cyclical theory of continuity, so that death is merely a temporary state in a continuing process of births and deaths.
- A theory of *karma* that postulates one's present condition as being determined for the most part by the ethical nature of one's past actions.
- A theory of the nature of existence, known as *samsara*, which includes all living things in a circle of endless continuity.
- A theory of salvation (*nirvana*), the salient characteristic of which is the view that salvation (*moksha*) must involve the cessation of rebirth and must therefore occur outside the whole cycle of continuity or samsara.

d. A "Typical Text"

The "typical text" I would use to exemplify this doctrine is from the *Chandogya Upanisad.* I chose it because it is fairly detailed, as well as for other reasons which I will mention later.

> Those who, in the village, reverence a belief in sacrifice, merit and almsgiving – they pass into the smoke (of the funeral pyre); from smoke into the night; from the night into the latter half of the month, into the six months during which the sun moves south – ward, into the world of the fathers; from the world of the fathers into space; from space into the moon. That is King *Soma*. That is the food of the gods. The gods eat that.
>
> After having remained in as long as there is a residue (of their good works), then by that course by which they came, Into space, from space into winds.

> After having become wind, One becomes smoke. After having become smoke, he becomes mist.
>
> After having become mist, he becomes cloud. After having become cloud, he rains down. They are born here as rise and barley as herbs and trees, as sesame plants and beans. Thence, verily, indeed , it is difficult to merge, for only if someone eats him as food and emits him as semen, does he develop further.
>
> Accordingly, those who are of pleasant disposition here – The prospect is indeed that they will enter the womb of a Brahmin, or the womb of a Kshatriya, or the womb of Vaisya. But those who are of stinking conduct Here – the prospect is, indeed, that they will enter a stinking womb, Either in the womb of a dog, to the womb of a swine or The womb of a chadala (outcaste).

e. Some Comments on the Texts

Notice how the whole vision of rebirth or reincarnation, as it is also commonly called, is situated within a context of a general observation of the cycles in Nature. Given the fact of so much rebirth and cyclic development in Nature, it is quite logical to assume that even human life comes under the sway of such a cycle of rebirth.

We also note the incorporation of the whole system of caste into the scheme of reincarnation. Thus the quasi divine sanction is given to a possible given vested interest interpretation of the social set up. The Purusha-Sukta myth of the emergence of the caste, in the Rg Veda , was most likely a poetic attempt to express the interdependence of social groupings in society, so that none would be given superiority of inferiority. It is an irony of history that the Rg Vedic text has been given this oppressive interpretation and taken into the later Scriptures for further consolidation.

The chronology of the different passages (smoke to night to latter half of the month and so on) should not be taken literally and be made cause for ridicule. They are probably a poetic depiction of how things are inter-related, change, rise and fall in the various cycles of nature.

f. Some Critical Comments on Reincarnation

Like most views concerning the afterlife, reincarnation is not a scientific truth that can be rationally proved. If it is accepted , it must be accepted on faith, on reasonable risk, that is, by showing that there is *some* positive evidence (though not conclusive) in its favour. And if it is to be rejected, it could only be because one is averse to some of its implications.

Among the most striking "invitation to believe" in reincarnation is the fact that Nature, as a whole is cyclic. Besides, there is evidently a kind of "reincarnation" going on in the plant world. We plant seeds and from these grow cereals and, when we replant a grain of , say, wheat, it sprouts again and bears fruit. Reincarnation recognizes a certain basic interconnectedness in all of reality, including humans and their world. There is also a cycle of season and day seems to follow night along with a kind death and resurrection of the sun. It is interesting to note that *karma* and rebirth can be (and often is) upheld within a atheistic worldview: there is no need to postulate a divinity who would apportion successive reincarnation. *Karma*, in such a case, is seen as a kind of impersonal cosmic law – the " Iron Law of *Karma*", some call it – like the law of gravity, which binds all or reality together: " As you sow, so shall you reap!" Nor can it be denied that this belief has served to deter many a would-be bully or oppressor.

"If we are all reincarnations and have lived before, how come we have no memory of our former lives?" so runs the popular objection. It is an undeniable fact that by far the vast majority of us have no recall of how we lived in which former lives and so do not know for exactly what faults of our we are being punished, or for what good deeds we are being rewarded. But some do, we are told . the blood and thunder American General Patton was quite convinced that he had lived before. He even claimed to have remembered battles in which he had fought as an ancient Greek warrior. And, from time to time, in the popular press (especially in India) we read of a child in some remote village who suddenly speaks a language of a place it has never visited or recalls details about real people, still alive, whom it has never met. And haven't we all had, from time to time, a sense of *déjà vu* (literally, 'already seen')? The awareness that a place we've never visited is beginning to feel "vaguely familiar" or that an event is- coming across to us as a "repeat performance"? True, most recollections of former lives can be shown up for what they are: frauds perpetrated on a gullible group of people, with the hope of publicity and, perhaps even, monetary gain. And psychologists suggest alternative explanations for *déjà vu* that would not warrant such a far-fetched credence as the doctrine of reincarnation. But, when all is said and done, there *does* remain a baffling residue of cases that defy all other explanation, that seem to be quite authentic, no matter how demanding an investigation is let loose on them. There is the famous case of Bridey Murphy and others, well documented by men of science and doctors of no mean repute, who can be shown to be far from gullible and real "hard nuts to crack"! Some of these can be found by consulting the most interesting and carefully checked study of Dr Ian Stevenson, M. D., *Twenty Cases Suggestive of Reincarnation*.

Finally, reincarnation is, as I have said, an undeniably possible theodicy! It is another way to respond to the scandal of suffering in this world. It has a plausible answer to why some babies are born impaired or deformed or handicapped, why bad things happen to good people and vice versa : it's all a matter of retribution for the sins of ones former life. And rapists, extortioners and murderers who seem to be having a jolly good life in spite of their evil ways, well, they better watch out: in their next life, they'll have to pay for it in plenty!

g. On the Other Hand...

Reincarnation involves a rather dichotomised view of the human person, one in which, as I have said, the body is of totally secondary significance and not really part of the self. If that kind of understanding of the human person doesn't bother one, that he/she could accept reincarnation without batting an eyelid. But if, like me, you see the body as an integral of your make-up," such that you cannot be "you" with another body, just as you cannot be "you" with another "soul", then, like me, you would have problems with reincarnation. It is true that we do perceive a tremendous psycho-somatic union in our person such that psychic wounds can result in physical (somatic) maladies and somatic "healings" can be "suggested" to us by psychic influence, but "reincarnationists" would be able to find some way of explaining this while still retaining their body-soul dichotomy (even if I am not convinced by their reply). What is certain is that reincarnation is quite incompatible with an integrated view of the human person, one that sees the tangible aspect of me (my "body", roughly), as essential an element in my make-up as the intangible (the "soul" or psychic dimension).

And there's another difficulty I have with reincarnation: it tends to make oppressed people resigned to their lot, as has been the case with dehumanised untouchables (today's *dalit*!) and maltreated women. Reincarnation, thus (at least to traditional-minded people) offers a very strong dose of "opium": they must not rebel against their lot or fight for their "rights". Nor should social activists, philanthropists and revolutionaries campaign for the liberation of these people and the betterment of their miserable situation. By so doing, we are preventing these unfortunates from expiating their past *karma* and necessitating that they be born in a similar cruel and pitiable situation in the future ... if not in an even worse one; so as to atone for those unremitted sins! It cannot be denied that the theory of *karma* and of reincarnation has been one of the reasons why so many Indians have remained in a deprived, exploited condition with scarce a murmur of protest. In passing, it might be worth noting that for some people the very fact of having been born a woman is, in itself, a punishment for faults in ones previous life. Had one been really bad, he/she would have been reborn as a pig or a dog; being born as a woman implies being born into a slightly higher state. According to such people, in order to attain salvation (*moksa*). it is not enough to be reborn as a Brahmin, but a *male* Brahmin!

GLOSSARY

Agapeic: Agape (Ancient Greek ἀγάπη, agapē) is a Greco-Christian term referring to love, "the highest form of love, charity" and "the love of God for man and of man for God". The word is not to be confused with philia, brotherly love, or philautia, self-love, as it embraces a universal, unconditional love that transcends and persists regardless of circumstance. It goes beyond just the emotions to the extent of seeking the best for others. Religions like Christianity and Judaism are agapeic religions. Buddhism and Hinduism, despite their gnostic core, does not lack an agapeic element, and Christianity, despite its agapeic core, does not lack a gnostic element. Those who are Christian do not for that reason lack a gnostic dimension; those who are Buddhist do not for that reason lack an agapeic dimension.

Albigensianism: A Christian movement considered to be a medieval descendant of Manichaeism in southern France in the 12th and 13th centuries; characterized by dualism (asserted the coexistence of two mutually opposed principles, one good and one evil); was exterminated for heresy during the Inquisition. It is a modified form of the Manichaean heresy. Also called Catharism.

Algazel or Ghazali: Abu Hamid Al-Ghazali was one of the most prominent and influential philosophers, theologians, jurists, and mystics of Sunni Islam. He was of Persian origin.

Code: Code or Conduct covers the rest of the territory of religion: it stands generally for the behavioral requirements that the program of our religion lays upon us, but specifically for the moral aspects of those requirements. It forms the total activities and behaviours expected of a religious group.

Creed: Creed encompasses everything we think (or believe, to use the word loosely) when we undertake the program of a particular religion. Such thoughts may involve subjects as diverse as God, money, Satan, or jogging for your health. They may amount to nothing more than vague attitudes of approval or disapproval, or they may entail subscription to entire body of formal doctrine.

Cult: Cult stands for all the liturgical practices our religion's program calls for. These can range from chicken sacrifices at dawn, to Morning Prayer and Sermon on Sundays, to not eating saturated fats, to transcendental meditation, to owning a house in the Hamptons. At first glance, this spectrum of practices may look like nothing more than individual preference at work; but in fact, the particular "liturgies" we engage in are almost always dictated socially, by the community.

das Heilige: Rudolf Otto (25 September 1869-7 March 1937) was an eminent German Lutheran theologian, philosopher, and comparative religionist. He is regarded as one of the most influential scholars of religion in the early twentieth century and is best known for his concept of the numinous, a profound emotional experience he argued was at the heart of the world's religions. While his work started in the domain of liberal Christian theology, its main thrust was always apologetical, seeking to defend religion against naturalist critiques. Otto's most famous work, *The Idea of the Holy*, was first published in German in 1917 as *Das Heilige - Über das Irrationale in der Idee des Göttlichen und sein Verhältnis zum Rationalen.* It was one of the most successful German theological books of the 20th century, has never gone out of print, and is now available in about 20 languages. The first English translation was published in 1923 under the title *The Idea of the Holy: An Inquiry into the Non-Rational Factor in the Idea of the Divine and its Relation to the Rational.* Otto felt people should first do serious rational study of God, before turning to the non-rational element of God as he did in this book.

das Kreaturgefuhl: Otto describes the 'creature-feeling' in the following words: "It is the emotion of a creature, submerged and overwhelmed by its own nothingness in contrast to that which is supreme above all creatures."

Docetism: In Christianity, docetism is the doctrine that the phenomenon of Jesus, his historical and bodily existence, and above all the human form of Jesus, was mere semblance without any true reality. Broadly it is taken as the belief that Jesus only seemed to be human, and that his human form was an illusion. This view is important in Gnosticism.

Emanation: The origination of the world by a series of hierarchically descending radiations from the Godhead through intermediate stages to matter.

Eulabela. See Eusebeia.

Eusebeia*:* (Greek: εὐσέβεια from εὐσεβής "pious" from εὖ *eu* meaning "well", and σέβας *sebas* meaning "reverence", itself formed from *seb-* meaning sacred awe and reverence especially in actions) is a Greek word abundantly used in Greek philosophy as well as in the New Testament, meaning to perform the actions appropriate to the gods. The root *seb-*

(σέβ-) is connected to danger and flight, and thus the sense of reverence originally described fear of the gods.

Ex nihilo: *Ex nihilo* is a Latin phrase *meaning* "out of nothing". It often appears in conjunction with the concept of creation, as in creatio *ex nihilo*, *meaning* "creation out of nothing", chiefly in philosophical or theological contexts, but it also occurs in other fields.

Future shock: *Future Shock* is a 1970 book by the futurists Alvin and Heidi Toffler, in which the authors define the term "*future shock*" as a certain psychological state of individuals and entire societies. Their shortest definition for the term is a personal perception of "too much change in too short a period of time".

Ganz Andere: wholly other. In this famous book "Das Heilige" (1917) by Rudolf Otto, who says that God is "das Ganz Andere." This implies that God is by nature distinct and different from us (not the immanent God).

Gnosticism: A prominent heretical movement of the 2nd-century Christian Church, partly of pre-Christian origin. Gnostic doctrine taught that the world was created and ruled by a lesser divinity, the demiurge, and that Christ was an emissary of the remote supreme divine being, esoteric knowledge (gnosis) of whom enabled the redemption of the human spirit.

Hierarchical structures: Hierarchy is a way to structure an organization using different levels of authority and a vertical link, or chain of command, between superior and subordinate levels of the organization. Higher levels control lower levels of the hierarchy. You can think of an organizational hierarchy as a pyramid. The best example of hierarchical structure is the Church.

Hierophanv: (from Greek hiero-, "sacred," and phainein, "to show") is a term designating the manifestation of the sacred. The term involves no further specification. Herein lies its advantage: It refers to any manifestation of the sacred in whatever object throughout history.

Hominisation: The process of becoming a human being.

La chanson de Roland: The Song of Roland is an epic poem based on the Battle of Roncevaux Pass in 778, during the reign of Charlemagne. It is the oldest surviving major work of French literature and exists in various manuscript versions, which testify to its enormous and enduring popularity in the 12th to 14th centuries.

Laity: Ordinary people, as distinct from professionals or experts (or clergy).

Lotos-Eaters: "*The Lotos-Eaters*" is a poem by Alfred Tennyson, published in 1832. The land of the Lotos-eaters seems to be stuck in some kind of endless afternoon, and the speakers of the poem are obsessed with eternity, death, and endless sleep. It sounds like a hoot. Over the course of the poem, we lose track of when and where we are.

Mana: (in Polynesian, Melanesian, and Maori belief) an impersonal supernatural power which can be transmitted or inherited. It is a dynamic supernatural power or influence dwelling in and flowing from certain individuals, spirits, or things and capable of producing great good or evil

Manichaeism: was a major religion founded by the Iranian prophet Mani in the Sasanian Empire. Manichaeism taught an elaborate dualistic cosmology describing the struggle between a good, spiritual world of light, and an evil, material world of darkness. They were adherents of the dualistic religious system of Manes, a combination of Gnostic Christianity, Buddhism, Zoroastrianism, and various other elements, with a basic doctrine of a conflict between light and dark, matter being regarded as dark and evil.

Manichees: see Manichaeism.

Massa damnata: Augustine of Hippo (354-430) taught that Adam's sin is transmitted by concupiscence, or "hurtful desire", resulting in humanity becoming a massa damnata (mass of perdition, condemned crowd), with much enfeebled, though not destroyed, freedom of will.

Masters of suspicion: "School of suspicion" is a phrase coined by Paul Ricœur in Freud and Philosophy (1965) to capture a common spirit that pervades the writings of Karl Marx, Sigmund Freud, and Friedrich Nietzsche, the three "*masters of suspicion*".

Mocrobes: A microorganism, especially a bacterium causing disease or fermentation. The term 'microorganisms' include bacteria, fungi, viruses and protozoa.

Motor immobilis: Latin for immovable mover, normally designated as the Creator God.

Mvsterum tremendum: See Tremendum et fascinans.

Mystery: See problem.

Myths: Myths are symbolic stories which throw light upon who we are, where we are heading and how we "fit in" to the scheme of things. However, "modern" we may be and however much our generation may have "come of age" - particularly if it is a highly technocratic society that we have grown up on - we need to cultivate and feel a "sense of belonging." And that is precisely what a functioning myth does.

Nausea (French: *La Nausée*): It is a philosophical novel by the existentialist philosopher Jean-Paul Sartre, published in 1938. It is Sartre's first novel and, in his own opinion, one of his best works. It can be seen as the forerunner of Sartre's existentialism, which he was going to formulate in his work "Being and Nothingness" in 1943.

NDE: A near-death experience (NDE) is a personal experience associated with death or impending death. Many people report seeing a bright light at the end of a long dark tunnel after a near-death experience.

Niebelungslied: The Nibelungenlied, translated as The Song of the Nibelungs, is an epic poem from around 1200 written in Middle High German. Its anonymous poet was likely from the region of Passau.

Nirguna: According to Adi Shankara, Nirguna Brahman is Para Brahman, and is a state of complete knowledge of self as being identical with the transcendental Brahman, a state of mental-spiritual enlightenment (Jnana yoga). It contrasts with Saguna Brahman which is a state of loving awareness (Bhakti yoga). According to Advaita as taught by Sankara, saguna brahman refers to the Lord identical with his own infinite jnanam. Sankara refers to him by names such as Shiva, Vishnu as specified in the vedas and upanishads.

Numinous: Something numinous has a strong religious quality, suggesting the presence of a divine power. When you enter a temple, church, or mosque, you might feel as though you've entered a numinous space. Numinous comes from the Latin numin-meaning "divine power."

Oscar Romero: Saint Óscar Arnulfo Romero y Galdámez was a prelate of the Catholic Church in El Salvador who served as the fourth Archbishop of San Salvador. He spoke out against poverty, social injustice, assassinations, and torture amid a growing war between leftist rebels and government and right-wing forces. He was assassinated on 24 March 1980, while celebrating the Eucharist.

Panentheism: the belief or doctrine that God is greater than the universe and includes and interpenetrates it. It is opposed to pantheism, which believes that everything is God. (meaning "all-in-God", from the Ancient Greek πᾶν pân, "all", ἐν en, "in" and Θεός Theós, "God").

Pre-determinism: The view that the outcome or course of events is determined in advance by divine will or fate; predestined. Determination. It also implies that one's salvation is predetermined by God.

Priesthood, cultic: A *priest* or priestess is a religious leader authorized to perform the sacred rituals of a religion, especially as a mediatory agent between humans and one or more deities. A cultic priest is one who focusses on the exact celebration of the ritual. Cultic priesthood is opposed to the prophetic priesthood, who as spokesperson of God tries to bring about change in the society.

Privatio boni: The absence of good (Latin: privatio boni) is a theological doctrine that evil, unlike good, is insubstantial, so that thinking of it as an entity is misleading. Instead, evil is rather the absence or lack ("privation") of good.

Problem: The distinction between problem and mystery is one that hinges, like much of Marcel's thought, on the notion of participation. "A problem is something which I meet, which I find completely before me, but which I can therefore lay siege to and reduce. But, a mystery is something in which I am myself involved, and it can therefore only be thought of as a sphere where the distinction between what is in me and what is before me loses its meaning and initial validity." Again: "When I am dealing with a problem, I am trying to discover a solution that can become common property, that consequently can, at least in theory, be rediscovered by anybody at all. But…this idea of a validity for "anybody at all" or of a thinking in general has less and less application the more deeply one penetrates into the inner courts of philosophy." Marcel often describes a mystery as a "problem that encroaches on its own data."

Prophet: The Prophet (literally, a spokesperson) has not so much a rubric to execute as a message to proclaim. The prophet can be of any sex, social group or community. Whereas the priest's role was usually understood as to coax a whimsical divinity to do as he directed, the prophet's function was seen as just the opposite: interpreting God's word and, thence, calling the people to action and change of heart.

Purusa-Sukta: According to some scholars, the origins of the caste system are found in the poem, Purusha Sukta, in the 10th book of the Rig-Veda, whose ten books are generally judged as dating back to the second half of the second millennium b.c.e. In the Purusha Sukta, the four chief castes – the Brahmin (essentially, the religious/philosophical/teaching/scholarly sector), Ksahtriya (essentially, the political governing and warrior sector), Vaishya(sp.?) (essentially, the commercial/economic sector), Sudra (essentially, the service sector) – are pictured as having come from the Lord's mouth, arms, middle and feet, respectively.

Quinaue viae: The quinque viae (Latin "Five Ways") (rarely called "five proofs") are five logical arguments regarding the existence of God summarized by the 13th-century Catholic philosopher and theologian St. Thomas Aquinas in his book Summa Theologica.

Religare: Many say the etymology of religion lies with the Latin word religare, which means "to tie, to bind." This seems to be favored on the assumption that it helps explain the power religion has

Sa-guna: See Nirguna Brahman.

Sarna: Instead of artificial structures, the tribal people make use of a natural shrine – the sacred grove, or *sarna.* as it is called in India. Tribals tend to have a very close-knit social set-up: everyone feels responsible for everyone else and the poor, orphans, widows and the ages are taken care of, very lovingly, by the whole community.

Sat-cit-ananda: Satchitananda or Sacchidānanda representing "existence, consciousness, and bliss" or "truth, consciousness, bliss", is an epithet and description for the subjective experience of the ultimate, unchanging reality in Hinduism called Brahman.

Sophia: The Ancient Greek word Sophia (σοφία, sophía) is the abstract noun of σοφός (*sophós*), which variously translates to "clever, skillful, intelligent, wise". These words share the same Proto-Indo-European root as the Latin verb sapere (lit. "to taste; discern"), whence *sapientia*. The noun σοφία as "skill in handicraft and art" is Homeric and in Pindar is used to describe both Hephaestos and Athena.

Summa Theologiae: The *Summa* Theologiae (written 1265–1274 and also known as the *Summa* Theologica or simply the *Summa*) is the best-known work of Thomas Aquinas (c. 1225–1274). Although unfinished, the *Summa* is "one of the classics of the history of philosophy and one of the most influential works of Western literature."

Surplus of meaning: A "*symbol*" must have a "*surplus of meaning*"-as opposed to an ordinary item. A *symbol* must be an expression of something (Saussure) and it must be recognizable (Peirce) or participate in the depth dimension of reality (Ricoeur).

Surrogate victim: As René Girard reflected on religious symbolism and the rituals that present and enact it, these constitute ways of simultaneously commemorating and masking the real collective violence and victimization that gave rise to human society. His *Violence and the Sacred* argued forcefully for the universality of this fundamental cultural force: "All religious rituals spring from the surrogate victim, and all the great institutions of mankind, both secular and religious, spring from ritual. . . . It could hardly be otherwise, for the working basis of human thought, the process of 'symbolization,' is rooted in the surrogate victim".

Symbol: Ricoeur defines 'symbol' as any structure of signification in which a direct, primary, literal meaning designates, in addition, another meaning which is indirect, secondary, and figurative and which can be apprehended only through the first. The best example of a symbol is the body, which represents and participates in ME. In this sense, the body is the symbol of the person I am (me). I cannot be accessed or experienced without my body. I am more than my body.

Telefinality: Pierre Lecomte du Noüy coined the term "tele-finality" to describe this "direction from afar." God's cosmic providence did not Involve him running alongside the process, as it were, giving it a push here and a nudge there. Nor did he map out everything like a clever computer programmer and then sat back, apparently, to watch the whole show unfolding along swift and efficient lines. As we said earlier, God set the goal (viz. hominisation), but let the evolutionary process find its way there by trial and error, something like the rain water pouring in torrents on a mountain top must find its way eventually to the bottom.

The Flies (French: *Les Mouches*): It is a play by Jean-Paul Sartre, written in 1943. It is an adaptation of the Electra myth, previously used by the Greek playwrights Sophocles, Aeschylus and Euripides.

Tirthankaras: The word *Tirthankara* signifies the founder of a tirtha which means a fordable passage across the sea of repeated births and deaths. A *tīrthaṅkara* is an enlightened being who has conquered *saṃsāra* (cycle of birth and death), leaving behind him a path for others to follow. Jainism recognizes the following twenty-four *tīrthaṅkaras (ford-makers).*

Torah: The law of God as revealed to Moses and recorded in the first five books of the Hebrew scriptures (the Pentateuch).

Totemism: system of belief in which humans are said to have kinship or a mystical relationship with a spirit-being, such as an animal or plant. The entity, or totem, is thought to interact with a given kin group or an individual and to serve as their emblem or symbol. In the Elementary forms of religious life, Émile Durkheim seeks to show that society is the soul of religion – that society is the foundation of all religious belief. Religion has its origins in totemism. Totems are collective symbols that represent both god and society.

Transformism: This is a kind of concessional view of evolution and, indeed, Darwin's doctrine was a kind of transformism. It limits the evolutionary process to living beings only and excludes any human evolution from the process because of a particular conception of the human soul. Thus, we have universal transformism which upholds the passage from one primitive cell to the human body (but not "the. soul: that is held to be created separately by God either at, or some time after, conception) and then there is mitigated transformism which restricts itself to an acceptance of a separate development of each species by itself.

Tremendum et fascinans: Rudolf Otto, a German theologian, wrote The Idea of the Holy to describe how human beings experience God. For Otto, rational thought proved insufficient for understanding fully our experience of the divine. The supernatural reality of God Otto described as Numinous. (*Numen*, in Latin, means "God," or "spirit," or "divine.") The Numinous is far more than our sensory or rational processes can tell us, for the Numinous is "Wholly Other." God is far more than a cosmic-sized human being. Otto's description of how we know and experience the Numinous brings us to my beloved Latin phrase. We experience God, Otto says, as *Mysterium tremendum et fascinans*. Most simply, God is the unfathomable Mystery before whom we are awestruck and stand trembling, yet find ourselves inexorably drawn into relationship, attracted and fascinated in ways we cannot fully explain. A frequent source of awareness of God is found in sanctuaries of worship. In many such places, the grandeur of the architecture, the ominous drone of the pipe organ, and the divergence from ordinary day-to-day experience instill a sense of creatureliness, an awareness of being in the presence of God. In spite of being moved to awestruck reflection on the boundless glory of God, we are further transported into experiences of joyful praise of the love and grace of God, carried by the melodies of the organ to combine our voices in harmony with the worshipping community. When we have listened for a word from God and have experienced his presence, the feeling may subside, and we return to ordinary pursuits, although changed through our experience of the Numinous, the experience of God.

Vorgriff (transcending anticipation): This Vorgriff is inherent in human nature and by means of this anticipation, a person is capable of asking questions of being. ... To speak of a person as self-transcendent means that the person is able to reach out to that which transcends it – indeed, to the infinite ground of all reality (Karl Rahner).

Wish-fulfilment: Sigmund Freud (1856-1939) regarded God as an illusion, based on the infantile need for a powerful father figure; religion, necessary to help us restrain violent impulses earlier in the development of civilization, can now be set aside in favor of reason and science. Freud's psychoanalytic perspective viewed religion as the unconscious mind's need for wish fulfillment. Because, people need to feel security and to absolve themselves of their own guilt, Freud believed that they choose to believe in God, who represents a powerful father-figure. So, some atheists believe that humanity invented God out of need - to cope with the uncertainties of a confusing and often dangerous world. The psychological explanation for God is one of the most common arguments against Christian faith (and against any theistic religion). Belief in a god is common to all cultures in all time periods. Atheists prefer to explain this as "wish fulfilment" – that humanity invented God because we *wished* God existed.